Joseph D Simms

Soul-Saving

Or, life and labors of Henry M. Willis, evangelist and missionary, embracing an account of the revivals in which he labored in America, and of his missionary work under Bishop Taylor in Africa, together with a sketch of the life and work

Joseph D Simms

Soul-Saving

Or, life and labors of Henry M. Willis, evangelist and missionary, embracing an account of the revivals in which he labored in America, and of his missionary work under Bishop Taylor in Africa, together with a sketch of the life and work

ISBN/EAN: 9783337308797

Printed in Europe, USA, Canada, Australia, Japan

Cover: Foto ©Lupo / pixelio.de

More available books at **www.hansebooks.com**

SOUL-SAVING

—OR—

LIFE AND LABORS

—OF—

HENRY M. WILLIS,
Evangelist and Missionary,

EMBRACING AN ACCOUNT OF THE REVIVALS IN WHICH HE
LABORED IN AMERICA, AND OF HIS MISSIONARY
WORK UNDER BISHOP TAYLOR IN AFRICA,

Together with

A SKETCH OF THE LIFE AND WORK OF MRS ANNA WILLIS,
HIS WIFE AND THE COMPANION OF HIS TOILS, WITH
AN ACCOUNT OF HER EVANGELISTIC WORK
SINCE RETURNING FROM AFRICA.

—BY—

REV. JOSEPH D. SIMMS, A.M.,
Of the Central Ohio Conference,

With an Introduction by

REV. WILLIAM JONES, M B
Of the St. Louis Conference.

———

"He that winneth souls is wise."

To Ossian Simpson Willis,

THE ONLY CHILD OF

Henry M. & Anna Willis,

A boy tenderly loved, and the subject of many prayers; who in early childhood accompanied his parents in their Evangelistic work, from State to State, and finally "To Afric's Sunny Clime."

This Book is dedicated with the hope that Ossian, in future life, will serve the great cause in which his father so earnestly and faithfully labored.

"The earth and the sea shall give up their dead."

Preface.

The brief life of Henry M. Willis, evangelist and missionary, is ended. His career, though short, was intense and very successful. Few men, in such a short time, have so impressed themselves upon the world and accomplished so much in the Lord's work. Many are the souls that now point to him as the agent under God in their conversion. Many are the strong churches over the land that have received impulse and inspiration by his magic touch, and that date their larger prosperity from the time that he came to labor among them.

It will not be forgotten that he and his companion were the first missionaries stationed by Bishop Taylor in central Africa.

The original object of this volume is to collect and arrange in some connected order the main events in the life of our deceased Brother Willis, so that the book might be a sort of memoir or biography of his life and labors, and at the same time a presentation of his methods in gospel work. To this end materials were gathered by his wife, and the writer was requested to undertake the task of giving them form and order for the eye of the public. But it was apparent that such a task would not be completely formed without embracing some account of the life of his wife, Mrs. Anna Willis, who was his helper in all the main events of his public service, both in the evangelistic and missionary fields, and who now goes forward, according to her own desire, and the request of her dying husband, to fields of other and earnest evangelistic endeavor.

The work of Mrs. Willis, during the life-time of her husband, was so inseparably connected with his, that a book describing the service of one must, in some measure at least, set forth the work of the other. It has therefore been thought best to make this volume not only a memoir of Brother Willis, but also to include a sketch of the life and work of his surviving companion.

In the midst of the duties of a new pastoral charge and without opportunity to give such time and pains as a volume of this kind would justly demand, the writer has consented to undertake the work of this memoir and biography. He does so under such circumstances from two or three considerations.

The work has providentially come to his hands. During a large part of the public life of Brother Willis, the author had a pleasant acquaintance with him and had opportunity to study his plans of work. It had been suggested to Brother Willis that some account of his life and work should be given to the public. Some floating ideas had been entertained in his own mind that possibly some good might be accomplished by a work of the kind. If such a book were ever written Brother Willis desired that he who now undertakes this biography should write it. Accordingly after his death his faithful wife desiring to carry out the mind of her husband placed this task in the hands of the writer.

Without any pretentions to literary merit, the Author undertakes this work, unsought but providentially placed in his hands, with pleasure, because in so doing he may do a kindness and discharge an obligation due to an ardent friend and may, also, give expression to his own appreciation of the character and work of one who was so devoted and true to God.

The life and deeds of him of whom we are to write were of such a character and importance as to be noteworthy in the eyes of the people and deserving of publication in permanent form. The Author has long been of the opinion that no book should be written without some worthy object in view and unless some demand would be met by its publication that is not exactly supplied by any other. The eventful life of our deceased Brother Willis, and that of his surviving companion still engaged in public services and achieving great victories in the Lord's work, has created a place for such a work as is herein contemplated.

Many persons have already expressed a strong desire that such a book should be written, and that the events and plans of work in the career of our worthy and devoted brother and sister should be written, so that the life and services of these persons whom God hath raised up and honored at home and abroad by a succession of splendid victories may be known to all other christian workers, and to the world in general.

And may it not be that in accepting the providentia work of recording the events of these successful lives that good may be accomplished. Certainly the many letters and kind words of encouragement that have come to the Author since undertaking this work have confirmed him in this hope and helped him to the belief that in this respect his labors will not be in vain, but rather that good may be done and the Lord's cause advanced, and that the services herein mentioned and the successes grouped, in the life of Brother Willis, may prove an inspiration to others to offer themselves to the work of Christ and thereby fill up the ranks made vacant by the falling ones who may have gone forth to the great conflict for souls.

With these thoughts prominent and with acknowledgement of much aid rendered by Rev. J. H. Barren, Rev. J. K. Shaffer, Rev. Thomas Harrison, Prof. Robert F. Y. Pierce, Rev. E. D. Witlock, D. D , and others who have contributed valuable help in preparing these pages, we send this volume forth with the hope that it may aid in extending the knowledge of the Lord's work, and many hearts may be induced to make bolder and greater efforts in the Master's vineyard, and that God may be honored and His kingdom in the earth more rapidly advanced.

J. D. SIMMS.

Wauseon, Ohio, August 17, 1886.

Contents.

INTRODUCTION.

CHAPTER I.
Birth.—Parentage.—Family.—Home-Life.—Early Days.—Education and Youthful Character.

CHAPTER II.
Christian Experience.—Religious Advantages.—Influence of Home.—School and Sunday-School.—Conversion.—Begins Religious Work.—Joins Church and Y. M. C. A —General Christian Usefulness.

CHAPTER III.
Self-help and care for Others.—Business Career.—Aptitude in Worldly Endeavors.—Way opens for future Success. Religious work while in Business.—An Offer of Higher Wages.—A Call in another Direction.—Weighing the Matter.—"Three Days in the Tomb."—Decision.—Baptism of the Spirit.—The Gift of Faith.

CHAPTER IV.
Ready for Duty in the Lord's Work.—Work in the Tabernacle.—Decides to be an Evangelist.—Fields Open.—Past experience Beneficial.—Madison.—Unionville.—Geneva, a striking Incident.—Call to hold a Camp-meeting.—Call to Secretaryship of Y. M. C. A.—Licensed to Exhort and Commended by the Church.

CHAPTER V.
Camp-meeting at Lakeside.—Enjoys meetings under Harrison.—Meets Miss Anna Ruddick, an Evangelist.—Like Spirits.—Like Work.—They vow to Agree.—Two Engagements, one to Miss Ruddick and one to hold a meeting at Andover.—Is Married.—Two Evangelists unite for one Work.

CHAPTER VI.
A Leaf from his Wife's History.—Her Birth.—Parentage.—Early Education.—Religious Experience.—Missionary Tendencies.—Evangelistic Work.—Great success in Soul-Saving.—Called the Girl Preacher.—Missionary Opportunities.—Marriage.

CHAPTER VII.
First Revival Service after Marriage.—They two lay Siege to Andover.—Both ends of the Yoke Sustained.—Woman is a help-meet for Man.—The Work owned of the Lord. A wonderful Meeting.—WILLIAMSFIELD, a Short Meeting with deep Interest.—62 Conversions.—Church greatly Strengthened.—ORWELL, Grand Success.—Earnest Work.—Lord with his People—Mighty to Save.—Nearly 300 Saved in 16 Days.—Time of Refreshing.—Infidel Club Converted.—SPARTA, Deep Feeling.—People Confounded.—Awful Struggle.—Wrestling in Prayer.—Grand Victory.—A Hard Case.—Blessing in the Morning.—Christmas Day.—Powerful Sermon on "Strive."—End of 1882.

CHAPTER VIII.
Rest at Ashland.—Engaged for Tiffin, O.—The Preparation.—The work begun by Pastor.—Evangelists add Fuel to the Flames.—It Sweeps on.—Business men Visited.—Bell rung and Prayers offered at 12.30 P. M.—Effects Elecirical.—Power of God on the City.—Children's Meetings, Organizing a Class of 200 Children.—An old

Fashioned Demonstration of Power.—A Strong Man Prostrated.—Overflow of Attendance.—The work goes on until nearly 600 are Saved.—A marvelous work of God.—After the Revival.—Its work substantial, Conversions Continue.—The Church finished.—The promise of Revival fulfilled.—A Delightsome Land.—NORWALK, The fire Kindles.—Consecration and Prayer.—Crowds Gather.—Conversions Begin.—Fast Day.— A Precious Feast.—Altar Crowded.—182 Conversions.—Incidents of the Meeting.—Strength Failed.—Meeting Closed, and Evangelists seek Rest.—Go West on a temporary Visit.

CHAPTER IX.

Seeking Rest and Health.—A few days at Lawrence, Kan.—Attends Conference at Hiawatha.—Call to State Work.—Returning to Lawrence, Kan.—Received many calls to hold Meetings.—Little work is Undertaken.—Call to Marysville, Kan. is accepted.—The work entered upon.— House Overflowing.—160 Conversions.— The Church quickened.—Mrs. Willis conducting after Services.—Other Churches strengthened.—Extracts from the Papers.—People from ten miles away in Attendance.—The Bride and Groom from the Prairie Converted.—Results of the meeting Good.—Testimony of the Pastor.

CHAPTER X.

Abilene, Kan.—On way, discovered by a Pastor.—An unprecedented Eulogy.—Invited to tarry and hold Revival Services but was engaged for Abilene.—On Account of his wife's health could undertake no More.—Successful work and some remarkable Incidents.— Formalism receives a hard Blow.—Church membership without Salvation.—A rich experience and a Grand Testimony.

CHAPTER XI.

Returning to the East.—Rents a furnished cottage in Republic, O., in June, intending to rest for the Summer.—Bro. Guard invited him to Melmore.—He cannot be Hid.—The cry of souls is Heard.—Holds a two weeks meeting at Melmore.—A Wonderful Revival in Harvest Time.—More than 100 Conversions.—NEVADA, Called by the Presiding Elder to fill the Pulpit at Nevada.—Traveling a Circuit till Conference as a Supply.—He preaches in the Streets.—The White Horse.—Crowds hear him from his Carriage Pulpit.—Delivers up his charge at Conference.—Visits other Conferences.

CHAPTER XII.

Invitations received.—Wonderful cry for Evangelists.—Sometimes 300 Invitations Ahead.—He accepts Hicksville.—The Correspondence.—The Situation.—Hard pounding both Ways.—Holding on by Faith.—In Darkness.—Soon the Heavens were Light.—The great Victory.—The Holy Ghost fell on All.—The meeting Time.—The great deep broken up.—Sinners crying and Converts Shouting.—An Editor Saved.—A time of Rejoicing.—The beginning of greater Prosperity.—CAREY, O,—The Altar Filled.—The cry of Agony.—Salvation comes.—The crowds too Great.—An old man taking Christ on testimony and is Saved.—Numbers added to the Churches.—Pastor Taneyhill.—Upper Sandusky.—A two week's Engagement.—Bro. D. Cook, Pastor.—Three score of substantial Converts.—God owns his workmen, and the work moves on.

CHAPTER XIII.

LIMA, O.—Pastor Davies in charge of a great Church invites Evangelist Willis.—Much work ahead.—Hard Fighting.—The awakening spirit on the City.—Crowds

Attend.—Scores are Converted.—One Hundred and Thirty-Six decide for Christ.—FOSTORIA, O.,—Jonathan and his armor Bearer.—The Church at Ease.—The Few.—Pastor and Evangelist.—Earnest Work.—Pulling out of the Fire, 125 plucked as Brands.—The Church greatly Revived.—STRYKER, O.—A Few Days.—The Fire is Kindled.—Sins confessed and forsaken.—Estranged hands clasped in Friendship.—Sinners seeking Salvation —A Glorious Time.—April 20, 1884.—The work finished in the West.—The Season of Rest and Retirement.—A Few Months Vacation and Rest from the Strain of Revival Work at Tiffin, Ohio.

CHAPTER XIV.

PHILADELPHIA, PA., October, 1884.—Again in the Field.—A Call to be Assistant Pastor in the City.—Salary Offered.—Opening Prospects.—Accepts Evangelistic Work in West Philadelphia with Rev. Clark, Pastor.—A Good Meeting.—NORRIS SQUARE.—Rev. Thomas Harrison, Pastor.—Providential Opening.—Evangelist Willis invited.—First Night 51 at the Altar.—Victory.—The Good Work continued.—More than 200 converted.—Another Account.—The Work and Workers appreciated.—The Last Revival of Brother Willis.

CHAPTER XV.

How to succeed in Soul-saving.—Some Fail.—Mr. Willis always Won.—His Preparation.—Consecration and Acceptance.—Endued with Power.—Assurance of Success.—Peculiar personal Endowment.—Methods of Work.—Faith of the Church.—Earnest, Intense and Continued Prayer.—Fasting.—Work for All.—Power of Song.—Use of Tracts.—Mention of Good Done.—Fearless Preaching.—Expect immediate Results.—Open the way for Seekers.—Rejoice with the Converts.

CHAPTER XVI.

The Missionary Impulse.—Correspondence with Bishop Taylor.—The Sacrifice required. The self-surrender to work in Africa.—The Pledge demanded.—The Engagement for Work in Africa.—The Brooklyn Convention.—His Usefulness There.—An Inspiration to the Convention of Missionaries.—Account of Manager Rev. J. D. Griffin.

CHAPTER XVII.

Departure for Africa.—The Voyage.—Entertainments on Shipboard.—Storm in crossing Atlantic.—Arrival at Liverpool.—Kindness of Fowler Brothers.—On board Steamship "Biafra."—A Coast Storm.—Mrs. Willis' protracted Illness.—Kindness of Friends—Madeira Island.—Sierre Leone.—Conversion of Mr. Wilson.—A Wedding at Sea.—Kru boys.—Meeting Bishop Taylor.—Landing at Mayumba.

CHAPTER XVIII.

The Steamer leaves Mayumba.—Temporary Home with Mr. Evans.—Sunday Morning Services in Mr. Evans dining-room.—Visit to Mamby.—Mr. Willis and Ossian attacked with African fever.—A visit to the Native Villages.—A visit from King Mamby and many Natives.—Customs of the Natives.

CHAPTER XIX.

Bishop Taylor urged to request Mr. and Mrs. Willis to return to America.—The request made and accepted.—The arrival of the North bound coast steamer "Biafra."—The kind offer of Captain Thomas of the "Biafra."—Mr. Willis's farewell "palaver."—Anchored at Old Calabar.—Mr. Willis again attacked with African Fever.—The course of the vessel ordered far out to sea.—Brother Willis fast losing his hold on life.—His last words.—

His death and burial at sea.—Mrs. Willis almost crushed with sorrow.—Kindness of Captain Thomas and his officers and men.—Arrival at Liverpool.—Took passage on steamship "Servia" for New York.—Arrival at Philadelphia.—Memorial Service to Brother Willis.

CHAPTER XX.

Memorial Window—The kind people of Norris Square M. E. Church.—Mrs. Willis' stay in Philadelphia.—Her visit to the Methodist Episcopal Ministers' meeting.—Resolutions of sympathy.—Mrs. Willis departs for the home of her parents in Ohio.—The death of her father-in-law—The end of the history of the subject of this Memoir.

CHAPTER XXI.

Mrs. H. M. Willis.—By Nature an Evangelist.—Her gifts known to her Husband.—His dying request for her to continue the Work.—Her safe return to America.—The Salvation of Souls dearer than life.—Her brief Rest.—The opening of the Way.—Calls to Evangelistic Services.—NORRIS SQUARE, signal success.—Fever and Prostration.—Rest and Recovery.—Ready for Duty.—NORTH WALES, a Good Meeting.—TRINITY, NEW YORK.—Her Impressive Sermons—Her Modesty and Simplicity.—The Wonderful Display of God's Power.—A Glorious Revival.—Her return to Ohio.—Greets her Boy.—A Short Rest.—Returns to Philadelphia.—North Fourth Street Union Mission.—Anywhere to save souls.—The Pastor's Report.—The Jubilee Service.—Rejoicing and Testimony of many Converts.—Mrs. Willis greatly appreciated.—An Account of her Life Work.—Suffers still from African Fever and Nervous Prostration.—Compelled to rest.—Cancels many Engagements.—Returns to Ohio for the Summer.—Attends Summer Assemblies.—Expects to continue the Evangelistic Work.—Closing Remarks.

Introduction.

In the language of Dr. Talmage "I am requested to stand in the vestibule and open the door of this volume for the people." This task has some very pleasant and enjoyable aspects; and it imposes some duties that lie heavy upon the heart. To speak in a becoming spirit of the dead is not always an easy task, and to speak in the proper spirit and to say the right word of him whose lifeless form the deep sea covers, and to speak in the presence of her, who survives the death of her husband with sufficient courage to care for her fatherless boy and go forward and tell the story of the Savior's love, requires a pure motive and a discriminating mind.

Of him who, with fidelity to the facts and with finish of narrations, has undertaken the arduous task of collecting and collating the facts and incidents in the life of a friend whose career was so brilliant, yet so brief, whose sun rose so brightly, ascended to its zenith and sank so suddenly in the west, we can speak freely. It is eminently proper that I should extend this courtesy to the writer of this volume. For a term of years we were members of the same conference. When just from the University we had the extreme pleasure of entertaining him at the parsonage for a number of days and then driving with him in our own carriage across the country and introducing him to the good christian people of his first charge, and it is with a good degree of pleasure that we stand now on the threshold of this new enterprise and introduce him to the multitudes who will read his garnered store of rare trophies from the life and labors of him whose sun went down while it was yet morning.

The story of the evangelist, must of necessity, treat of evangelism. We believe in the true evangelism of the Church, having no confidence in any form of evangelistic effort which ignores the Church of God "which he purchased with his own blood." We cannot acquiesce in the sentiment that all evangelistic effort is to be discarded by the Church. For the accomplishment of the divine purpose "God gave some apostles, and some pastors, and some prophets, and some evangelists." And these agencies all combine "For the perfecting of the saints, and for the work of the ministry," and for the edification and enlargement of the Church.

God designed the Church for a noble purpose, and in order to reach that exalted position it must not only be pure, but it must take on such proportions as will enable it to stand perfect and complete in the "measure of the stature of the fullness of Christ." The fact that improper persons have entered the evangelistic ranks, lies with no more weight against the office of an evangelist than does the fact that improper persons in all ages have crept into the ministerial office, lies against the office and work of the ministry. The spirit that would exclude the evangelist from the field and abolish the office because some have not been true men, would close every pulpit in the land, and hush forever its warning voice because it has been disgraced by some unworthy of the sacred calling.

Neither can it be truly alleged that evangelists are the only promulgators of heresy in the Church. There are those everywhere who openly, in the exercise of their ministerial office, take delight in presenting phases of doctrine not found in the standard works of their own Church. Men are not to be received as infallible because they are ministers, nor rejected as the heralds of heresy and dissension because they are in the evangelistic work. The office of an evangelist is as wide in its application and effort as the functions of the ministry, and admits of as great diversity of talent in the fulfilment of its mission.

As no two men were ever alike in every particluar, no more can two successful evangeists be the same in method or manner—each one must of needs be a law unto himself. After years of severe and sometimes unkind criticism, Rev. Thomas Harrison has had one of the most successful years of his life. God has vindicated his claim to the office and exclusive work of an evangelist by giving him thousands of souls as the fruit of his labors. Rev. James Caughey was an evangelist owned of the Lord; cosmopolitan in spirit and labors, his were the steps and voice of a giant; thousands on both sides of the Atlantic were converted through his instrumentality, and eternity alone will reveal the extent to which his labors spiritualized the protestantism of the world.

We distinctly remember the evangelistic efforts of some persons we knew in childhood —some obscure laymen—the results of which stand to-day as a monument to their memory. I do not believe God will ever suffer the Church to fall into such a state or prelatical domination as to exclude special evangelistic effort. The publication of this volume will doubtless contribute to the accomplishment of this end.

As these pages will be read by thousands of earnest christians, old and young; as they shall follow H. M. Willis from his boyhood home in Northern Ohio, from the scenes of conflict and victory in his evangelistic campaigns in the east and west, to his last field of labor in the " Dark Continent "; as they shall contemplate his successes and look upon the strong, spiritual Churches that are the result of his labors, and see the host of strong men and women raised up by his effort, who still remain as monuments of his God-given efficiency, they will perceive that it was a divine hand leading him, and that divine power was the source of his success.

It is seldom a man projects himself so far into the future in so short a time, as did the subject of this volume. He was engaged in his work for only a few years; like the son of Elizabeth, "His was a brief period." He did not aspire to greatness, he did his work promptly and with a single purpose. He appears to us as if he might have adopted as the motto of his life:

> "I live for those who love me,
> For those I know are true;
> For the heaven that smiles above me,
> And awaits my spirit too;
> For all human ties that bind me,
> For the task my God assigned me,
> For the bright hopes left behind me,
> And the good that I can do."

Henry M. Willis belongs to that class of public workers who knew by intuition the way to the hearts of men. He startled the sensual and the careless by the suddenness and boldness of his assault. He was not great in the sense in which some of the great preachers won distinction. He was neither like Summerfield nor Maffit. He belonged rather to a class of lay workers. He sustained such a relation to the great preachers as some of the minor prophets sustain to Isaiah and Daniel. He was like Micah or John the Baptist, breaking out from the regions of obscurity and rousing the people to a tempest of anxiety for salvation. He was not a comet whose gorgeous train filled all the heavens with its mighty glow; he was a meteor blazing for a moment in the sky exploding by its own velocity, but instead of going out in darkness, leaving all the moral heavens tinged with the brightness of his radiance.

The surviving companion of the subject of this volume was Miss Anna Ruddick. If she was not born an evangelist, she was inducted into that office by the Holy Ghost at her conversion and confirmed and ordained by the same authority through the experience of full salvation.

Early in the career of Henry M. Willis these youthful laborers met and being mutually attracted, were soon united in marriage which proved a very happy union; and it is difficult now to determine to what extent her influence affected his career. To us at a distance, she always appeared as an essential factor in his work, a proper climax to all his efforts. She did not revolutionize him; she did not change his manner or modes of thought. She was an augmenting force; she was the central sun that, by the law of spiritual gravitation, kept him in his orbit; and yet they were one—the two hemispheres of one orb—in their work they were essential to each other.

This volume must, in a measure, represent the evangelism of H. M. Willis with his living co-operating environments and it must in a large degree represent Rev. Joseph D. Simms, the ardent friend whose fascile pen records the achievements of one, who, having finished his brief but victorious career, died on ship-board and was buried in the sea, while his sorrowing but triumphant companion survives him with sufficient strength and courage to carry on the work for the Master.

Read this story of the pure, self-sacrificing, heroic, christian worker from the pen of the chaste and scholarly author; read it carefully and prayerfully; it will quicken every religious impulse and add a thousand fold to your purpose to be better and do more for God and humanity.

WM. JONES,
Sedalia, Mo.

CHAPTER I.

Birth.—Parentage.—Family.—Home-Life.—Early Days—Education and Youthful Character.

Henry Milton Willis was born in Ashland, Ohio, July 17, 1858. His parents were Dedrick W. and Sarah A. Willis.

He was the third of nine children, having four brothers and four sisters, two of whom, an older and a young brother died in infancy. Henry was the oldest son that grew to manhood.

His parents were both natives of Pennsylvania. His father was born in Lancaster County, March 22, 1829; and his mother in Washington County, February 2, 1828. They were married at Wooster, Ohio, March 20, 1854, and at once located permanently at Ashland, Ohio. Here Henry's father engaged in business, and for some years was a tin merchant, in good pecuniary circumstances, owning stock and real estate.

But through misfortune or misplaced confidence his business failed, his means were soon exhausted, and he was left penniless. Failing to succeed in business and determined to support his family honestly, he next engaged in farming fields in the suburbs of the place, and in doing many other kinds of hard work. For the successful endurance of which his constitution was quite inadequate. Grief on account of loss of property and overwork, entirely broke down his health and took away his courage, so that he became, in the later years of his life, a helpless and dependent invalid, and died of his chronic ailments August 31, 1885.

He had been an excellent provider for his household, a kind, loving and thoughtful husband and father, who had bright plans for the well-being of his family and the education of his children, but with loss of property and health his brightest earthly hopes for helping his large family were completely thwarted, and instead of helping others, he himself needed to be helped.

From early life he was a member of the Dunkers, or Brethren Church, and always sought the religious welfare of his family. Henry's mother, still living at Ashland, Ohio, is of the same religious persuasion, and her pious life and example have been greatly felt in the moral and religious training of the children. Henry greatly loved and appreciated his mother.

His father being an invalid and without means for several years before his death, the support of the family fell upon the older children, the oldest of which was a daughter, Susanah L. Willis, afterwards wife of Rev. A. A. Mead, of the North Ohio Conference. She taught nine years in the public schools of Ashland, supporting herself and contributing to the support of the family.

Henry, being the oldest son that grew to manhood, assumed his full share of the responsibility when quite young, and never failed to make money and assist in providing for the wants of the family at home to the end.

Notwithstanding the long affliction of the father, the Willis home was attractive, and a kind, heavenly Father sustained and raised up help in their every financial need. The children grew and helped each other and helped the parents. The home was a center of healthful christian influence, where all the children delighted to be.

The mother always made home attractive for the little folks by providing something for

their edification and entertainment. She lived
with reference to the welfare of her children,
and to this end her motherly influence was
directed. They were permitted to have their
plays, and at the evening hour would listen to
stories, counsels and conversations of the parents, and would spend much time in singing.
Family worship was held and much attention
was given to religious culture at home. The
children were taught to pray and to exercise
strong faith in God. Although reared in town
these children were seldom on the streets, but
under the firm, patient hand of a christian
mother, the home became an attractive training
school. The boys were reared to manhood
without any taste for the streets, the card-table,
the dancing-hall, the drinking saloon, or tobacco
in any form, but all grew up to embrace the
christian faith, and to be living witnesses of
Christ's power to save. The girls grew to pure
womanhood, adorned with the grace of christian character.

Under these healthful home influences Henry
Willis, the subject of this sketch, began his
early days. He entered the public schools at
Ashland, at the age of six. He was a bright,
obedient, studious and faithful pupil in every
particular from the beginning, especially gifted

in mathematics and languages with unusual ability for drawing and music. He pursued the course of study in the public schools until he reached the higher grades, when he was obliged to leave school on account of home finances, which now he must aid in providing.

He cheerfully left school to engage in the hard labor of farming; but his evenings would be spent in study. He played the organ and sang as he had opportunity; often the last sound at night, in his boyhood home, was his voice in song together with the organ. Early in the morning he would sing hymns of praise. He was never a person who would murmur or complain, and even in sickness he was quiet and patient and ever employed.

At one time, in his boyhood, when confined to his bed on account of a severe lameness, his hands were busy and among other things, which he did, was the knitting of a large rug for his mother. He always delighted to help his mother; and was very industrious at all times. Even when farming, he would take his leisure of the noon hour to engage in the exercise of singing, and playing the organ. He was always punctual and precise in his doings, not very communicative, but rather reticent and reserved as a boy, but always very generous and kind. From early life he gave a certain large portion of his income for the welfare of others. Giving was a part of his religion, and benevolence a prominent characteristic of his entire life.

CHAPTER II.

Early Christian Experience — Religious Advantages. — Influence of Home, School and Sunday-school. — Conversion. — Church and Y. M. C. A. — General Christian Usefulness.

In this chapter we furnish the following account from the pen of Rev. J. H. Barron, of the North Ohio Conference. He speaks from personal knowledge, and thorough acquaintance with the early life of Brother Willis, and is well qualified to furnish the readers with as correct information as any that can be given. He has written at this point of the history as follows:

The early life of Rev. H. M. Willis was characterized by uncommon vivacity and quickness of perception, and by an unvarying love of that which was religious.

He grew up to manhood under the religious training of a mother who was a pious woman and a member of the society called Dunkers.

His school privileges were of the best afforded by the village. Here again were influences thrown around him of a religious character, such as reading of the Scriptures, and prayer by the teacher, and song and praise by the school.

These devotional exercises had their desired effect upon the minds of the pupils and kept before them the necessity of a personal religious life.

In the Winter of 1876, a revival meeting was begun in the old Methodist Church, in the village of Ashland, under the direction and labors of Rev. Samuel Yourtee. These meetings were attended by christians of all denominations, and were especially successful in the conviction and conversion of the young people.

With many others who were led to the altar was Harry Willis, who, while bowing before God, repented of his sins, "with that repentance which needeth not to be repented of," and with an earnest heart and a broken contrite spirit he " sought and found " forgiveness of all his sins, and arose from the altar with a consciousness that he was a child of God The dark night of sin and condemnation which had rested upon his soul, was dispelled by the dawning of the Day Star from on high; and he was enabled to say with the Psalmist— "The Lord is my light and my Salvation."

This was February 2, 1876, being the anniversary of his mother's birthday.

Having been a regular attendant upon the Sunday School and a member of a large class of young men, he immediately went to work for the Master, seeking them out through the large congregations that assembled night after night; he greeted them with the message with which Philip greeted Nathaniel: "We have found Him of whom Moses, in the law, and the prophets did write, Jesus of Nazareth, the son of Joseph." Like the bee that has found a satisfying supply of honey, fills itself, and then goes with delight and strength to tell others of its sweetness and source; so he went telling to all around what a dear Savior he had found.

And many were the trophies of Grace which he found for the Lord Jesus Christ through his earnest and prayerful labors, in that series of revival meetings.

After the close of the Winter Campaign Harry found in the church and in the Y. M. C. A. channels for enlarged usefulness. Then began in him the cultivation of a large charity, which was ever after the peculiar characteristic of his life.

Presbyterians, Lutherans, United Brethren, Baptists, Methodists, all who loved his Savior were loved by him.

He attended religious services, carried on by different denominations, and was always welcomed by them as an earnest, faithful and useful young man.

His delight, next to that of communion with Jesus, seemed to be in communing with his Saints. These hallowed associations were always a delight and a pleasure to him, and from them he derived spiritual power. He proved the words of the prophet, "They that wait upon the Lord shall renew their strength, they shall mount up with wings as eagles; they shall run and not weary, and they shall walk and not faint."

So he had a renewal of strength as each means of grace was attended and enjoyed.

Very early in his christian life it was noticeable that he was a "Chosen Vessel," that he was not to mark out his own course in life, but that God had his life-work already in waiting for him.

Not only had his lips been touched with a live coal, taken from off the altar, but his heart had received a living Christ. "The zeal of God's house had eaten him up." So when he heard the voice of God "Whom shall I send and who will go for us" and evangelize this world, bear the glad tidings of salvation to the lost and famishing of the earth, Harry's voice and heart, like that of Isaiah of old, cried out, "Here am I, send me." Though the riches and honors of the world just before me within my easy grasp, yet for the Lord and the saving of the lost, I turn my back upon them all, and cry "Here am I' ready to do what Thou wilt have me; ready to go whither Thou wilt direct me; ready to suffer all Thou shalt cause to come upon me; ready to encounter the greatest difficulties, fight in the hottest battles, wander in the most barren deserts, and die if needs be on sea or land, at home or among strangers, ready to have my grave where loved ones can come and visit it, and weave a chaplet of flowers and strew the early spring beauties upon it, or in mid ocean be lowered beneath the gurgling waves and find a resting place for this earthly house amid the moss and weeds that grow in the silence and depth of the blue sea. Such was the spirit and self-consecration, and anxiety for the work of Christ in the earth that led Harry Willis out into the work of an evangelist.

New opportunities and experiences were offered him in a new field of labor, which had opened for him in Cleveland, through the Y. M. C. A. of that city. Here he was permitted to join with those choice kindred spirits in the worship of God, in the frequent gatherings of all classes of christians in the delightful and beautiful rooms of the Y. M. C. A.

Here God was pleased to own his labors in the reclamation and salvation of multitudes of young men. Here he visited almshouses, hospitals and the lowest places of iniquity, seeking to lift up and save those who had fallen victims to shame and sin. All the sympathies of his nature seemed to be in this Christ-like labor, and often he rejoiced in God that He had thus led him to so broad a field of usefulness.

But this city was not to be his life-long field. After two or three years labor, here, through the providence of God he was thrust out as a traveling or itinerating evangelist

Traveling from village to village and from city to city, God putting His seal upon the labors of His servant, by permitting him to see hundreds in a single series of meetings, turning from the service of satan unto God.

And this was not to be wondered at. He was the sent of the Lord. His heart and sympathies beating in harmony with the heart of his Divine Redeemer.

He dealt openly, yet tenderly and prayerfully, with sinners. He gave the gospel trumpet no uncertain sound. While he told men of the guilt and power of their sins, he placed before them a Savior that was able and willing to save, not only from the guilt and penalty of sin but from the power, pollution and being of sin. One that could save to the uttermost, all that came unto God through Him.

Hence he became a power for good. God through him was mighty to the pulling down of the strong-holds of sin; and as deep as are the ocean waves that now roll over his mortal remains, so deep were the mighty waves of God's salvation that rolled over the communities, visited by the young soldier of the Cross.

He has passed from labor to reward; or in his own dying words, "into the Glory which is just ahead."

Having labored and walked with God he was not; for God took him.

Let his earnest, zealous, self-sacrificing life be an inspiration to every true christian, and may the influence of his holy efforts in the cause of our beloved Master be felt and perpetuated until the kingdom of this world shall become the kingdom of our Lord and Savior Jesus Christ.

CHAPTER III.

Self-help and Care for others.—Business Career.—Aptitude in Worldly Endeavor.— Way opens for Future Success.—Religious Work while in Business.—An Offer of Higher Wages. —A Call in another Direction.— Weighing the Matter.— "Three Days in the Tomb."—Decision.—Baptism of the Spirit.—The Gift of Faith.

Having improved the opportunities that were offered in his boyhood life, for attending school, and having reached the grade of the high school in education and self-improvement, the force of circumstances now imposed another question upon his young and thoughtful mind. It was that of financial self-support, and the necessity of aiding in the care and maintenance of the large family to which he belonged; and to whose support he must now contribute more than ordinarily falls to the lot of a boy, because of the financial losses and affliction that had in the mean time come to the family.

For the duty of self-support and care for others, he willingly left his school with its dear associations and privileges to engage, so young, in the stern realities and labors of life. He had already formed habits of study and was impressed with the idea of self-improvement, and never left off his studious habits. In after life he carried books with him and improved leisure moments in reading and study; but his school advantages were now at an end and he must turn to account his knowledge and strength to make them count in a more material form.

After leaving school Henry engaged for a time in farming fields rented by his father, who had now abandoned all mercantile pursuits to engage in the tillage of fields in the suburbs of the town. Serving thus at farming and other hard labors until the Spring of 1877, having attained the age of nineteen, he left the parental roof for the first time, to try his fortune elsewhere and in another line of business pursuits.

He first went to Glendale, Ohio, where he engaged as a clerk in a bakery for a short time. He next went to Mt. Pleasant, Hamilton County, Ohio, where he was employed as head clerk in the store of Henry Moser, one of the largest dry goods and general variety establishments of the place.

While at this place he had a Sunday-school class of grown persons and helped to take charge of the church music. Here he organized a society of the Y. M. C. A. and became its president. In many ways he assisted Pastor McLean in both town and country work. The work of the Lord was greatly revived during his stay. As a token of esteem in which he was here held, and in appreciation of his labors for this class, he was presented with a beautiful gold pen and holder. In the Winter of 1878, just before the holidays, he returned to his parental home at Ashland, Ohio. Here he engaged as a clerk for Mr. E. Sepper, a dry goods merchant of that place, until after the rush of the holiday trade, when he was employed to write in the office of Probate Judge, at the Court House.

In the Spring of 1879, he once more put his hands to the plow, and together with his brother George W., who was then a boy of 15 years, engaged in farming in the suburbs of Ashland. This was his last experience in farming. His father was now a helpless invalid. After this Henry began clerking for Mr. Worst in a grocery in Ashland, which afterwards became a large grocery and boarding house, known as the Centennial Store, with Mr. Austin as partner In this Henry was given charge of the most important business, such as receiving and marking goods, making arrangements, etc. This position he held for some considerable time until he resigned. He had by this time become a very successful clerk and salesman, and now many good offers were presenting themselves for his acceptance in the commercial world. In the Summer of 1880, he went to Cleveland, where he was employed for about a year as a book-keeper in a coal firm. Afterwards he took a position as a commercial traveler and salesman for the firm of Z. A. & R. Montgomery, manufacturers of woolen goods, at the Salineville Woolen Mills.

While at Cleveland and elsewhere, engaged in business, his love for the Lord's work was manifest, and in many ways he sought and found opportunities for christian work. In the Y. M. C. A. of Cleveland he found a delightful sphere of christian activity, and in many ways was employed by the association in its work of holding meetings, visiting almshouses, infirmaries, the docks, and in its general work and labor of love. When employed as a traveling salesman, it is said that young Willis would buy up his opportunities to work for the Lord. While on the road he sometimes would do in sixteen days, the work of twenty-four, so that he might spend the other eight days in special service for the great Master. Doing all this religious work and yet all the while prosecuting his business so thoroughly that his services were constantly in demand and opportunities for higher wages and better positions were presenting their tempting offers.

While prospering in a financial and business way, he never forgot to send largely of his earnings to parents at home, whose main support he had now become. He was ever a dutiful son and labored without a murmur or complaint; not alone for self care, but gave most of his earnings for the care of others.

While thus demonstrating his aptitude for worldly success and endeavor, earning good wages as a commercial traveler and doing in the meantime as much work for Christ as it was possible for one to do situated in like circumstances. He was beginning to feel, more and more, the claims of God upon him, as a chosen worker, and that these claims could not be set aside by anything less than to give himself and his whole time to the service of the Lord. The call sounded louder and it became evident that God had marked out for him, a different line of operation from that which he had chosen for himself and upon which he was now entering so successfully and for which he seemed, in every way, so well adapted,

It was about this time that he received a call from a firm in Pittsburg, Pa., with an offer of $500 per year more than he was now receiving. He went to that city to negotiate with the parties, and to engage in answer to the calls of business. But the impression of a call in another direction was growing deeper, and the fact that God had set him apart for himself was becoming more evident to his own mind. He could not rest and went to his hotel, but he became so worried that he was sick and prostrated. At this hotel, in his room, for three days the struggle went on. He was fighting the battle with God's special claim, and it was soon to be decided who should win in the strife. The call of a business career was before him with its offer. His father was an invalid and moneyless, and he was now largely responsible for the care of the family at home. To give up business and engage for Christ was the impulse of conscience and the voice of God. It might bring with it its poverty and weight of persecution and great things to be suffered for the name of Christ. But in this three days of awful struggle and self examination, which he afterwards characterized as his "three days in the tomb," the Lord triumphed gloriously. Young Willis surrendered to do the whole will of his heavenly Father, even to giving himself and his time entirely to his divine service; to go anywhere, to be anything or to do anything at the command of the Savior. No sooner was the decision made than the Holy Spirit came upon him in pentacostal power and he received the fullness of the blessing of the Gospel of Christ. He was filled with the Spirit—every chamber and court of his being. A special baptism for the work of the Lord had been given him, and now he felt himself in harmony with God and ready to obey. He felt however that there was one blessing which he might yet receive from God that would equip him for a life of soul-saving, and that was what he called the "gift of faith"; for this he earnestly. besought God, struggling all night in prayer. Toward morning, like wrestling Jacob, he had gotten the victory and prevailed. He was assured that to him was given a power of faith which was not the heritage of every true disciple, but which he like many especially equipped for God's work, had now received, exalting his soul into a realm where it had an unusual degree of power with God to prevail, and procure promised blessings, and also to have extraordinary power over spirits and spiritual influences. His faith ever afterwards was wonderful. He could now trust God fully and take him at his word, nothing doubting. It was ask, believe, receive. To seek was to find, to ask was to have confidence that he had the petition desired of him. Ever after this, the gift of faith, in this sense, he claimed as a possession, and which in certain states of mind, clothed him with almost irresistible power. Of this power we shall have occasion to speak in a subsequent chapter. He was from this time in the Lord's hands subject to orders from the King of heaven.

CHAPTER IV.

Ready for Duty in the Lord's Work.—Aid in the Tabernacle Work —Decides to be an Evangelist.—Fields Open.—Past Experience Beneficial.—Madison, Unionville and Geneva.—A Striking Incident.—Call to Hold a Camp Meeting.—Call to Secretaryship of Y. M. C. A.—Licensed to Exhort and Commended by the Church.

Having fully decided the great question of his life-work and concluded to forego the pleasures and profits of a business career to engage entirely in christian work, the Lord led him in a plain path and soon revealed to him that he must go forth and hold meetings as a traveling evangelist, to work for immediate results in soul-saving. This call he now gladly accepts and in this work he already had considerable experience. When yet in business and a member of the Y. M. C. A. of Cleveland, he was often sent out as we have seen, in the work of conducting revival services in various parts of the city, and towns adjacent; where it at once became apparent that he was especially adapted to conduct bible readings and hold Gospel meetings, to the saving of many souls.

In the People's Tabernacle of Cleveland he had often aided the Pastor in his Gospel work, and by whom he was highly prized as a young man of earnest deeds, ability and burning zeal in the cause of Christ. In a letter written after hearing of the death of Bro. Willis, the Rev. Wm. Johnson, pastor of the People's Tabernacle wrote saying:

"My acquaintance with dear Harry was quite intimate when he was here in the city, and I esteemed him very highly. He seemed to be such an earnest, consecrated young man that I was much drawn to him. He often helped me in my tabernacle work, and always seemed to be full of faith and Holy Spirit, and ready for any work the Master should indicate. I had marked out for my dear young brother a life of great usefulness. And so, of course, was shocked to hear of his early death in a foreign land."

Being set apart of the Lord and anointed for his special work, and it being known to some extent that his services as a young christian worker and evangelist were available, the

fields soon began to open before him. The
guiding hand of Jehovah was evident in opening the way, a fact that always holds true, that
when God has a work for us to do we may be
sure that he will open the way for us to enter.
Thus it was for the young and boy-like evangelist, Harry Willis. As soon as he was ready
for duty the way opened for earnest work, and
toward the latter part of 1880, he received and
accepted an invitation to assist in holding a
meeting at the Methodist Episcopal Church in
Madison, Lake Co., Ohio. This providential
opening and introduction of Brother Willis into
the evangelistic work is described by the pastor,
Rev. J. K. Shaffer, in the following words:
" My first acquaintance with Bro. H. M. Willis
was at Painsville, Lake Co., Ohio, in the
Autumn of 1880. Mrs. R—— was holding
service in Bro. Day's Church, and I had gone
up to attend it. I did not notice him in the
congregation although he was there. In the
morning at the station two young men entered,
one a lawyer and the other Harry Willis. Here
I was introduced to him. He was then engaged
in other business. Dr. Sheridan Baker was
coming to Madison and we needed some one to
conduct the singing. Apparently by accident
(but providentially) I found out that he could

play and sing. He was what I wanted and I invited him to Madison. He consented; the day was set. At the appointed time I started to the station and met him on the side-walk. I can never forget him. He wore a jaunty little blue felt hat, his gossimer thrown loosely around his shoulders and a grip-sack in his hand. His beautiful young face and sparkling eyes were very impressive. At first he seemed timid but that soon wore away. He became a companion for the children and they were delighted with him. Until this day they speak of Harry Willis as their ideal. Little Charlie says, 'Nobody could jump as far as Harry Willis.' It is scarcely needful to say that the meeting was a great success. About eighty or ninety professed religion, and the church from a low state was greatly quickened and has been growing in influence since. This was Dr. Baker's first acquaintance with him, and he ever after held him in high esteem. The good people of Madison remember him affectionately and often speak of him as the 'Boy Evangelist.'"

His next work was with the same pastor at Unionville, Ohio, a beautiful little town exactly on the line of Lake and Ashtabula Counties. At this place it was soon evident that the Lord was with him and that he went not out to battle in his own strength, for it was soon seen that the work was progressing and that there was a mighty outpouring of the Spirit of the Lord upon the church and people. Under date of February 2d, he was enabled to write to his mother, saying: "The altar and sometimes six or eight seats around it were filled with people seeking Christ and a clean heart. The work prospers and we are having mighty outpourings of the Holy Ghost." And in the same letter he says "It was a trial of my faith to give up a good position and take my chances in this work; but now I do not fear in the least. I have gotten over all worry and am going to leave all in the hands of the Lord. I am not afraid, but feel sure that he will take care of us all."

These meetings grew in interest from day to day, and under the blessing of God many were drawn to Christ and saved.

Mr. Willis here proved himself an earnest, able worker, drawing friends to himself, only to tell them of Christ and his saving power. The church, through his efforts was greatly revived and strengthened, and many young people and others were saved and led to join in the work of the Lord.

In all this great work he was not without some trials and opposition. It was here that one man swore that he would break up the meeting and carry the evangelist out of doors, and with a number of his boon companions came one night, evidently for that purpose; but the difficulty was more easily met than many imagined. Mr. Willis saw his man come into the church and with a courageous and loving heart ran down the aisle and threw his arms around his neck. The man immediately broke down weeping, and was led by the evangelist to the altar where he adjusted all matters with God and was soon gloriously converted. His antagonism was all gone and he had nothing more pleasing now than to join in the great work of the meeting, in bringing souls to Christ. Another conversion of the meeting was of remarkable interest. A wealthy infidel, from some cause, had offered $25 to Mr. Willis if he would come to the place and hold a meeting. As the work went on this man got under conviction, and had no peace or rest. He went away to Cleveland, seeking rest and relief from his distress of soul but found none. He was drawn to the meetings, could not stay away, came back to the service and went to the altar, where he earnestly sought and found that peace which the world can neither give nor take away. Afterwards he testified that when away he could hardly wait to get back to the meeting and get to the altar, that he might find his mother's God. After this he was ready to give another $25 to carry on the work. Thus God wrought mightily and in this early meeting crowned the labors of his servant with abundant success. A further description of this meeting we here give from the pen of Pastor Shaffer, as follows:

"At the close of our meeting at Madison we went next to Unionville. Dr. Baker went home. Bro. Willis attended a meeting of the Y. M. C. A. at Toledo, but with a promise of return. As the opening was favorable he came on and we held another blessed meeting. About ninety professed religion here. He led the meeting mostly himself. It reached old and young, big and little, families and individuals, the back-slider and the church-member, the moralist and the drunkard. A number of young men and women were saved. Some have since gone to heaven. The children were greatly delighted with their meeting and many professed conversion; indeed the whole town was revolutionized. At Unionville, Brother Willis remained most of the summer with Brother Lucian Gail, who became his fast friend. I never saw a man more knit to another; it was Jonathan and David again. He prepared him a room in his own home, beautifully furnished with hanging lamp, carpeted, bed, organ and book case. Here Harry stayed during the summer. The only condition was that he would occupy this as a home. He enjoyed it greatly and studied and rested, which he much needed. The people gave him a handsome donation and many beautiful presents, as an illustration of how affectionately he was held. When he left, Brother Gail came into his room and sat in the chair in which Harry used to sit and wept like a child. May two such friends meet together in heaven and dwell forever by the throne of God. Oh how he loved him, no word could tell it, his soul seemed to be wrapped up in that young man."

After this meeting at Unionville many invitations began to come to him to hold meetings and conduct revivals in various parts of the country. The churches seemed glad to welcome any one who had the Soul-Saving power and who under God could arouse religious interest and enlist the public attention. To some the propriety of evangelistic aid is not clear, and some pastors would forbid them. But the churches were hungry and wanted revivals, and would welcome any agency that God might raise up to win souls to Christ. Among other places that now opened to Mr. Willis to hold special revival services, was the M. E. Church at North Geneva, Ohio.

Here he began meetings about the first week in April, and continued seventeen days, closing on the 20th of the month. At this meeting Mr. Willis worked so hard that his strength failed him, and on account of which the services were closed much sooner than otherwise they would have been. He had not yet learned to husband his strength and to suitably adjust himself so as to endure the great labor demanded for a long seige of revival work. But success gloriously crowned the effort and 51 professed salvation, while to his mind it was clear that many more were within easy reach if the meetings could be continued. But on the last evening the evangelist was compelled by lack of strength to sit in his chair and conduct the services. And must seek the needed health for other opening fields of labor before him. From Geneva Mr Willis now returned to Unionville, where in a few days his health and strength much improved.

He is now solicited to remain at Unionville and assist the pastor, Rev. J. K. Shaffer, for the remainder of the conference year, which it appears that he concluded to do, and for three months was among the Unionville people, working, exhorting, lecturing, holding bible meetings and spending most of his time in study and preparing for his greater evangelistic work that he knew was just before him. Here, like John the Baptist, he was preparing to go forth to call men to immediate repentance. Here he had a delightful home and already had many friends warmly attached to him since the meetings held here in the February previous.

While located here many invitations kept pouring in upon him for his services as an evangelist and christian worker. One of these was to the state secretaryship of the Y. M. C. A.

Among others a request was one to hold a camp-meeting at Thomson Ledge, a most beautiful and picturesque place in Ashtabula County, eight miles from Unionville. But having on his hands the work at Unionville, and desiring to prepare himself for the Fall and Winter campaign as a regular evangelist, he undertook but little outside work during the Summer, and remained for the most part at Unionville, where he was amply supported by voluntary contributions of church and outside people. And at the close of his Summer work among them (about July 20, 1882) a splendid reception and donation was given him at the residence of Mr. and Mrs. Warner.

A correspondent of one of the papers writes of this reception: "He had by his earnestness, consistency, and geniality, endeared himself to a host of friends and admirers, who desired to express, in some material way, their respect and appreciation. As a slight token of esteem over forty dollars in cash were handed in. Besides the cash some valuable presents were made. Mrs. Hopper, though absent in Cleveland, sent ten dollars. Geo. W. Lawton donated a complete set of Channing's works, also a number of other very handsomely bound books, making eighteen volumes in all. Most bountiful and excellent refreshments were provided, and over one hundred were present. The best wishes of the whole community go with Brother Willis to his new fields of labor."

At this place Mr. Willis was recognized by the church as having gifts and graces for the Lord's work and was given license to exhort and exercise his gifts under the authority of the Methodist Episcopal Church. His first license was dated July 25, 1882, and signed by J. K. Shaffer, P. C. at the Unionville charge, Cleveland District, East Ohio Conference.

CHAPTER V.

Camp-meeting at Lakeside, Ohio.—Enjoys Meetings conducted by Rev. Thos. Harrison.—Meets Miss Anna Ruddick, an Evangelist. — Like Spirits. — Like Work. — They Vow to Agree.—Two Engagements, one to be Married, another to conduct a Revival Meeting.—Is Married.—Two Evangelists Unite for one Work.

From his Summer engagement at Unionville, Ohio, about August 1, 1882, he goes to Lakeside to enjoy the great camp-meeting to be held there at that time. For this meeting the services of Rev. Thomas Harrison, evangelist, had been secured. Already Mr. Harrison had become distinguished as one of the greatest soul-winners of the day. Everybody was anxious to see and hear him. Thousands came to Lakeside to enjoy the meeting under the great evangelist. Some came to see and enjoy, others to work and learn. Many persons wanted to see how souls were won, and how the masses of the unsaved could be saved so soon to the cause of the Lord. The meetings under Mr. Harrison were full of power from the very beginning. The high expectation that had been raised concerning his influence and work was fully met. Lakeside never before had enjoyed such a tidal wave of salvation. Conversions took place daily and in a few days hundreds were saved. The whole Tabernacle was sometimes converted into an altar for seeking souls. On one Sabbath morning the interest in seekers began in the love-feast, and became so great that the work of praying with souls desiring to be saved could not be remitted even to allow the regular preaching at eleven o'clock; but the altar services went on uninterrupted till after the noon hour.

No one attending these meetings, and co-operating in the work, was a more interested observer than Mr. Willis. He studied the philosophy of the work, and day by day he drank in the spirit of the genius who, under the power of the Holy Ghost, had set in motion, forces that resulted in such a wonderful religious movement. Here he beheld and studied closely the work of a master workman. It was indeed a school of instruction. He was a learner in the work of soul-winning, and from these meetings he, no doubt, derived an impulse and an inspiration that was to have its influence upon him in all his future work. He ever afterwards looked upon Mr. Harrison as the ideal of his class, as well as the original of a type and style of evangelists which afterwards appeared in the fields of the world.

While thus Brother Willis was enjoying and profiting by these meetings, another one alike interested in the Lord's work, was on the ground taking part; and becoming more or less prominent in the meetings, and especially in the department of the young peoples work.

This was Miss Anna Ruddick, daughter of Rev. C. E. Ruddick of the North Ohio Conference. She had come to the camp-meeting fresh from fields of Christian usefulness, and here her light could not be hid. The young christian workers coming from different parts of the country, soon were made acquainted with each other. In these meetings, amid these hallowed associations, Mr. Willis and Miss Ruddick met for the first time. They were like spirits, and their deep sympathies were the same in the one great work of God in the earth. They often met here in the christian work of the young people. Their acquaintance was mutually cultivated, and before the camp-meeting closed an attachment had sprung up between them never to be broken. From this time their acquaintance was kept up, and their hearts were indeed joined together.

After much pure and hallowed association together, and after much prayer on the part of both, it became evident to their own minds that God had intended them for each other, in the journey and work of life. It was a subject of deep consideration and devout prayer. They would not enter into the marriage relation unless it would be reverently, discreetly, and in the fear of God. After becoming satisfied that it was the will of the Lord, believing that God would bless their union to the furtherence of his cause, they vow to agree, and an engagement is made which is solemnly kept.

After Lakeside camp-meeting Mr. Willis retires to his old head-quarters in Cleveland for a few days, where among others he receives an invitation to hold a meeting at Andover, Ohio, a village in Ashtabula County. This he accepts and engages to commence services there in the following October. Until that date no other work is undertaken. Mr. Willis now reserves a few weeks to himself. These he spends among friends visiting for the most part, at his old home in Ashland, Ohio, during which time he attends the session of the East Ohio Conference, held at New Philadelphia, Ohio, within the bounds of which he had labored in his evangelistic and pastoral labors during the Summer. Here he received many invitations to evangelistic work and the way more clearly opens before him. The Lord leads in a plain path.

Two engagements are already made, and with much fidelity he is preparing to fulfil them. The time arrives for the consummation of his marriage engagement with Miss Ruddick. This important event takes place, according to previous arrangement, and Henry Willis is married to Miss Anna Ruddick, at the residence of the bride's parents, by Rev. C. E. Ruddick, father of the bride, at Republic, Ohio, October 12, 1882. They were now no more twain but one flesh and their work should henceforth be one. They were to engage together in the same service and under the same yoke. For ten days before the marriage they spent a great part of the time on their knees praying God's blessing on their proposed union, and that he would make them great soul-winners together. They take for their special promise through life, the words of Christ: "Again I say unto you, that if two of you shall agree on earth as touching anything that they shall ask, it shall be done for them of my Father, which is in heaven." God answered their prayer by giving them great success.

CHAPTER VI.

A Leaf from his Wife's History.—Her Birth.—Parentage.— Early Education.—Religious Experience.—Missionary Tendencies.—Evangelistic Work.—Great success in Soul-Saving. —Called the Girl Preacher.—Missionary Opportunities.— The Marriage.

Miss Anna Ruddick, whose marriage to Rev. H. M. Willis we have just noted, was born in Philadelphia, Pa., in the latter part of the year 1861. She was the oldest of four children, having two sisters, Ida and Lily, and a brother, Charlie, who died in infancy. Her father was born in New York, in 1837, and her mother whose maiden name was Read, was born in New Jersey, in 1838. They were united in marriage in the year 1860, in the city of Philadelphia, by the Rev. Jas. E. Merideth, of the Philadelphia Conference. Her father is a minister in the Methodist Episcopal Church, in the North Ohio Conference. He is a very active and untiring worker, and has been distinguished everywhere as very successful in winning souls. His present charge is at Mt. Hope, Holmes County, Ohio.

Anna's mother is a most devout and pious woman, and enjoys the full confidence and love of her household. Her influence and example have had great weight in moulding the character and religious life of her children. Anna would make special mention of her own early christian training, by faithful parents, as a factor in her preparation for future usefulness. From early life she was taught the principles of the christian faith, both by precept and example, and early learned to pray and love God. At the age of twelve she openly sought and found the Saviour and was sweetly converted. Some years before, her mother had attended a camp-meeting at Urbana, Ohio, where, under the labors of Alfred Cookman, she experienced the blessing of holiness. After her own conversion, Anna noticed a great difference between her mother's experience and her own. She herself, sometimes, gave away to impatience and anger. Her mother did not, but was ever cool and self-poised, with every power and passion under control. Anna thought a higher experience for herself was attainable and accordingly sought after it with all her heart. At about the age of fifteen, after a great struggle with herself, she was enabled to make a full consecration of all to God, as complete as any one could make in older life. She laid her young life, ambitions and hopes, talents and will on the altar, and felt assured that the altar sanctified the gift. From early life she talked of being a missionary when she should grow up, and anxiously waited for that time to come. With her full consecration there came a longing desire to do something immediately, and accordingly, she began doing whatever her hands found to do. The Master gave her little things to do here and there, and she found that in obedience was perfect peace.

About this time she attended a revival meeting at Berea, Ohio. One evening the pastor urged christians to go back in the congregation and work among the unconverted. She accordingly went down one of the aisles, trembling and feeling that she had no message for any one; but noticing a crowd of young students who appeared anything but serious, she stepped up to one and simply said "The harvest is great but the laborers are few," and turned away confused and troubled, and was told by Satan that she had made a dunce of herself. She went to her knees in prayer and cast her burden on the Lord. Some years afterwards while attending a camp-meeting a gentleman greeted her with a glad smile and asked her if she remembered speaking to a young student and simply saying, "The harvest is great and the laborers are few?" She told him that she well remembered it. He said that he was that young man, and that those words had led him to Christ. He had now become a minister of the Gospel, with a charge in the West where he had just had a great revival, leading many souls to Christ.

Between the age of fifteen and sixteen, Miss Ruddick first entered the evangelistic work. The occasion which called her forth into the work and opened the way, was a seeming necessity, and quite providential. Some gentlemen living about twenty miles east of Cleveland had called on her father to see if he could not go and hold a meeting in the church of which they were members. But her father was just recovering from a severe illness and of course could not go. Anna had been in her room praying for God to give her some special work to do for him; and when she found that these men must return without any help a strange inspiration seized her to go. She put the question to her father: of course he was astonished but did not dare to say no. She went with the men and that evening stood up for the first time before a congregation as a public speaker, taking for a lesson the first chapter of Galatians. The power of the Lord came down, sinners trembled, and believers were stirred and a great revival followed.

Not long after this meeting closed, Miss Ruddick received a call to Crawford County, Ohio, and together with Mrs. Foote, an evangelist, worked in the Swail Church successfully. God blessed their labors abundantly. From there she went with her papa to the Swamp Church, but he remained only a few days, leaving Anna to carry on the meetings. She was equipped with the might of God; night after night the church was crowded. The altar was filled with seekers for pardon and seekers for heart purity. In writing of those times in after years she says, " As I look back on those days it seems as though I knew very little about myself, and I lived more in heaven than on earth. I seemed carried along by a wonderful inspiration. God filled my mouth with messages and honored his own word. Glory to the Father and to the Son and to the Holy Ghost. People began calling me the girl preacher, but what mattered it to me what I was called so that souls were saved."

After a short visit at home she next went to labor in the M. E. Church at Ripley, Ohio, with Rev. Charles Russel, pastor. It was a repetition of the previous meeting just held, only greater in results. The church was continually crowded at the night meetings and people poured in from miles around to the house of God, until there was not standing room. Ministers were sanctified, long standing quarrels were made up, the church was revived and in about eighteen days some 150 were gloriously saved.

Her next engagement was with the Ripley Congregational Church, Rev. A. Leonard pastor, who had received the fullness of the blessing at the previous meetings. In writing of this meeting afterwards she stated that "It exceeded all the previous ones in power and results." The space between the first pew and the rostrum was so crowded with seekers that there was hardly room to work among them. Then followed engagements at Greenwich, New London, Shiloh, etc., all in Ohio.

When about seventeen, she became impressed that she could do more for the Master if she had a better education and accordingly attended school at Baldwin University, Berea, Ohio. When Anna reached the age of nineteen, her father was sent to Sand Ridge Circuit, North Ohio Conference. From this time she remained at home with the exception of holding two or three meetings, assisting her father, and in pursuing her studies until the happy marriage with Mr. Willis, evangelist, with whom she again entered the field.

The Missionary impulse followed her from childhood, and at a State camp-meeting, held at Mansfield, Ohio, when she was about sixteen, she met for the first time, Rev. Wm. Taylor, now Bishop, who observed her spirit and took her name for his future Missionary work. She has ever since entertained the most tender regards for Wm. Taylor. A pleasant correspondence afterwards was had between them until she, with her husband, engaged with him in the great enterprise of evangelizing Central and Southern Africa.

When a girl, about eighteen, the way also began to open for her in India. Dr. Thoburn had become acquainted with her and desired that she would go with him to India to engage there in evangelistic work, and he thought that the way would be open in about two years from that time. When the time came she received a letter from Mrs. Gen. Cowen, of Delaware, Ohio, sister-in-law of Dr. Thoburn, stating that the way was open and that they were ready for her to go to India, but at about that time she was married to Mr. Willis, an evangelist, who expected to labor in this country. And consequently for the present, at least, her life was turned in a different channel from that of the foreign work.

CHAPTER VII.

First Revival Service after Marriage.—They Two lay siege to Andover.—Both ends of the Yoke Sustained.—Woman is a help-meet for Man.—The Work owned of the Lord.—A Wonderful Meeting.— WILLIAMSFIELD; A Short Meeting with deep Interest.—62 Conversions.—Church greatly Strengthened. — ORWELL; Grand Success. — Earnest Work—Lord with his People.—Mighty to Save.—Nearly 300 saved in 16 Days—Time of Refreshing.—Infidel Club Converted.—SPARTA; Deep Feeling.—People Confounded —Awful Struggle.—Wrestling in Prayer.—Grand Victory. —A Hard Case.—Blessing in the Morning.—Christmas Day.—Powerful Sermon on " Strive."—End of 1882.

This engagement with Miss Ruddick now having been fulfilled, another that Mr. Willis had previously made with the M. E. Church at Andover, Ohio, to hold a revival series required a like fidelity.

Having now formed a substantial alliance with one experienced in the field of evangelistic endeavor and one in every way prepared to be a " help-meet for man," in full sympathy with the work of Soul-Saving he feels himself re-enforced and strengthened for the work before him, and is now all the better prepared to fulfil his engagements with the Church at Andover. No time is to be lost, " the King's business requires haste." Married at 12.30 P. M., and that very evening at six o'clock, accompanied by his bride, he starts for the field of revival work at Andover, in Ashtabula Co., Ohio. Arriving there according to previous arrangements, they were warmly received, and held their first meeting on the evening after arrival. Mr. Willis has now a true helper for this and for all his future work. For the most part he does the preaching and has charge of all the services, not excepting the singing. Mrs. Willis presides at the organ, seconds all the movements ordered by Mr. Willis and frequently conducts the afternoon meetings, and occasionally delivers talks and addresses through the meetings at other times. Where the stern and hard truths spoken by Mr. Willis sometimes wounds and afflicts, exposing sin and reproving wrong, the sweet accents of Mrs. Willis' voice easily point the way to the great remedy for sin. And the rough places are made smooth and the crooked paths made straight and the work moves rapidly on.

At Andover the people are at once attracted. Mr. and Mrs. Willis entered the work with the highest expectations of victory. The Spirit of the Lord is manifestly present from the beginning. The community is stirred and the meetings grow in interest. The excellent revival music has no small part in the success of the work. A choice selection of one hundred revival hymns arranged by Prof. T. C. O'Kane, called "Songs of Praises," and used in all the services of Mr. Willis, and rendered by the evangelist, soon became familiar and were sung with spirit and enthusiasm by the congregation, until they became a most attractive and inspiring part of the meeting. With much enthusiasm the work moves on, the revival spirit prevails, barriers are swept away, sinners are awakened and many precious souls are saved. A glorious victory in a very few days is wrought in the name of the Lord. Mr. Willis and wife are now ready for another place of work and on invitation, proceeded to Williamsfield, Ohio, a small town a few miles South, and in the same county, where they had just been engaged. On October 31, 1882, work is begun and meetings held daily except Saturdays until the 19th of November. At this place the success in soul-saving is still more signal. Almost from the beginning seekers began to present themselves, and conversions were reported daily and sometimes as high as twelve in a day. During this meeting on one Sabbath afternoon they went to Wayne, a small village near by, where Mr. Willis preached one sermon and held one service in the M. E. Church, when eleven arose for prayers and five came to the altar seeking Christ. Here they were solicited to stay and hold a meeting but decided not to do so. After a meeting of some eighteen days with continued success throughout, with conversions almost daily, until in so small a place sixty-two conversions were reported. On Sabbath evening these meetings are closed amid the prayers and tears of the many present at the services. A correspondent of a paper from Williamsfield writes, saying. "Mr. and Mrs. H. M. Willis, evangelists, have just closed a series of meetings at this place. They have done good work for Williamsfield. Many have been converted and the church has been greatly revived and strengthened. They leave many warm friends and many an earnest prayer will go up that God may bless them in other fields of labor as he has in Williamsfield. They go to Orwell next to begin meetings there, from which place we expect to report good things."

After a few days of rest and visiting among churches where they had held services, the church at Orwell, Ohio, is prepared for their coming. They commence November 29th, and lay siege to the citadel of sin and wage aggressive warfare in the name of Christ. For sixteen days the battle goes on, and each day, from the beginning, was a day of success for the Lord's cause. At the end of five days Mr. Willis writes to his parents, saying "we have held meetings here five days and in that time over one hundred have expressed a desire to be saved, and about seventy-five of them have been converted, and besides about seventy-five have expressed a desire for a clean heart. We are having glorious times." In the same letter Mrs. Willis writes, saying "pray very often for us, God is using us for his glory for which we praise him."

As these meetings went on there were some days of remarkable power, and demonstration of the spirit to reprove of sin and change the heart. On one evening an infidel club of an Eastern college hearing of the wonderful work that was going on under the evangelists, concluded that they would visit the meeting and accordingly sent word before hand that they were coming and wished Mr. Willis to meet them in debate after meeting. Without any promise however, on the part of Mr. Willis, one evening they arrived just after altar services had commenced. Mr Willis, as was his custom, was working his way through the congregation entreating the unconverted. People were falling upon their knees all over the church. The mighty power of God that could not be resisted was on the congregation. There were seekers from the door at the front entrance to the pulpit, and the whole church was an altar and a house of prayer. In his work of personal invitation, the evangelist came to the leader of the infidel club, who was sitting in the back part of the house, and whispered in his ear "are you saved?" The young man commenced to debate. Mr. Willis fastened his strong, piercing, black eyes upon him and asked again "are you saved?" The Holy Ghost had done his work of convincing and the young man fell on his knees crying for mercy and seeking salvation. Mr. Willis went on with the meeting inviting and urging others to be saved. After the regular meeting of the evening had closed instead of a debate with the infidel club, an after meeting was held and they all came to the altar seeking pardon in the name of Christ: and the most of the number were converted and went on their way rejoicing. Their spirit of debate was gone, the spirit of God had argued the case with each and won a signal victory.

At another time during the progress of the meeting a very wicked man, who had not been to church for years, was disturbed on account of the Boy Evangelist who was creating such a stir in the community. His family had been attending the meetings and one daughter had just been converted. He was incensed and provoked to anger when he heard of it, and on a bitter cold night turned his whole family out of doors for attending the meeting. At last, stimulated by the excitement that was moving the town, and drawn by an unseen power, he concluded one evening to go himself to see and hear the celebrated evangelists. He did so, and all through the services listened attentively, but sat looking very morose and sullen. Mr. Willis' theme, that evening, was "Eternity." He had preached with great effect and people were falling on their knees all over the house. As Mr. Willis was working in the congregation he came to this man and whispered the one word "Eternity." The man looked up and said, "What did you say that to me for?" Mr. Willis answered by asking him, "Where will you spend it?" The man left the church in anger saying that he did not believe that there was any such a word in the Bible and he was going to find out whether what he had heard from the evangelist was true or not. He found an old Bible and for about a week shut himself up hunting for the word Eternity. At last he found it, closed his Bible and went to church again. All these days the Spirit of the Lord was contending with him for a full surrender. And the word was nigh him even in his mouth, for he could not wait for the altar service but during the sermon he fell on his knees and was grandly converted. When Mr. Willis left the place this man followed him to the train and with tears thanked him for the change that the meeting had wrought in him.

This was truly a wonderful meeting, and in the short space of about sixteen days it was estimated that nearly three hundred had been converted. It was evident to ll that the evangelists labored with great earnestness, thinking of nothing more than the work of the great Master. The opportunities for the evangelistic services of Mr. Willis and wife were not wanting, but came in for greater numbers than they could fulfil.

From Orwell they go to hold a meeting at Sparta, Ohio. Over this charge Rev. G. F. Oliver was pastor, who was himself, a minister of no small revivalistic power, and a most earnest worker for Christ. He invited to his aid Bro. Willis and wife, who joined him heartily in the work of saving the town and community. On December 19th, the evangelists arrived and the meeting began. The time is short; for ten days the work went on. From the beginning most earnest prayer was made and upon the first invitation over thirty knelt to be prayed for. The people were astonished, and wondered at the work that was going on. A mighty struggle followed, and a great wrestling in prayer was required, until another victory was gained, and day after day the work went on with glorious results. Many sought to see Jesus. Among the seekers was one, the husband of a christian wife, who said he knew he was lost; and that he was the worst sinner that ever was. He wept, struggled, remained on his knees during three seasons of prayer. The struggle lasted all night but the blessing came in the morning. The next day was Christmas and on that day he gave his hand to the church under the consciousness that the blood of Jesus cleanseth and can make the foulest clean. "His blood avails for me."

"Though he was angry His anger is turned away and He comforteth me." The power of the Lord was displayed in converting and sanctifying grace throughout this meeting. Much emotion and weeping, expressive of deep feeling was often manifested, with result, corresponding to demonstrations made. On Sabbath morning, December 31st, the pastor, Rev. Oliver, preached a memorable sermon on "strive." In the evening Mr. Willis, to a crowded house, delivered his last message to this people, from Rev. 3:21; a very remarkable experience meeting closed the services for the day, and for the meetings, and brings them to the close of the year 1882.

CHAPTER VIII.

Rest at Ashland.—Engaged for Tiffin, Ohio.—The Preparation. —The work begun by Pastor.—Evangelists add fuel to the Flames.—It sweeps on.—Business men Visited.—Bell Rung and Prayers offered at 12.30 P. M.—Effects Electrical.— Power of God on the City.—Children's Meetings, Organizing a Class of 300.—An old fashioned Demonstration of Power.—A strong man prostrated.—Overflow of attendance. —The work goes on until nearly 600 are saved.—A marvelous work of God.—After the Revival.—Its work substantial, Conversions continue.—The church finished.—The promise of Revival fulfilled.

After a successful series of meetings closing at Sparta, Ohio, with the last night of the old year, Mr. Willis and wife spent a few days in rest and quiet with parents and friends at his old home in Ashland.

His next engagement is with the M. E. Church at Tiffin, Ohio, Rev. J. S. Reager, pastor. The field was an important and inviting one.

Tiffin, is situated at the junction of the B. and O. and I. B. and W. R. R., and in the oldest and one of the most beautiful districts of Seneca County, Ohio. It contains about 10,000 inhabitants, and is one of the most interesting and important cities in Northern Ohio. The church in this place had grown with the city; having a history since 1828, and now had a strong and substantial membership. This church edifice had several times been replaced by more convenient and more commodious house, until now they worship in a building, though incomplete, yet beautiful and of extraordinary size, and when completed, would cost $50,000. At this time the audience room was unfinished, and the congregation worshipped in the lecture room below, which is said to have been one of the most comfortable in the state.

Although this church had held its rank as one of the oldest and most influential churches of the place and had steadily grown; and had undertaken the building of such a magnificent church, yet their membership scarcely exceeded two hundred and fifty. And very little of the revival spirit was manifested, nor had a genuine, wide spread revival been enjoyed for many years. The previous pastor struggled with the spiritual situation and the last pastor endeavored to solve the revival problem by engaging the services of Rev. Thomas Harrison, the celebrated evangelist, who had just then won a grand victory, in Cincinnati. Tiffin was to be his next field of operation. His coming was awaited with much eagerness and even impatience. He appeared at the appointed time fresh from a field of grand achievements, and labored for a few days only; when from sickness or lack of support, he left the place to its fate and returned to his home in Boston.

The next year brought Mr. Reager to the charge; himself an untiring laborer in the line of revival work and soul-saving. He commenced a meeting in November, 1882, and for nine weeks continued the work with more or less success, winning a score or more to Christ, and prosecuted the work with commendable vigor. About January 8, 1883, evangelist Willis and wife are ready for duty at Tiffin, and report to the pastor, where they are very warmly and gladly received by Mr. Reager, who felt indeed that the Lord had raised him up help in time of need. Re-enforced by the coming of this efficient help the battle against sin and wickedness is renewed. The presence in the meetings of Brother and Sister Willis, who came unheralded, except that the daily papers announced the day before that Mr. and Mrs. Willis, evangelists, were to be in the city and would conduct the revival services at the St. Paul M. E. Church that Monday evening. It was enough, the house was full. A new impulse was given, fuel was added to the flames. Many expressed a desire for salvation and a number professed to be saved. Mr. Willis recorded in his diary of that day, saying, "Throat sore, hard work, fourteen for Christ. The people all very social and kind."

Day meetings are established, to be led mostly by Mrs. Willis, at 2.30 P. M. Also a children's meeting from four to five o'clock each afternoon. Mr. Willis and Pastor Reager spent the mornings in visiting and praying with the people, talking to business men in the stores and shops, exhorting and inviting them to Christ. The fire kindles more and more; the interest increases and the work revives. The house was soon crowded from night to night until it was understood, that if one would be sure of a seat he must go early. The spiritual results appeared as well as the crowds of people. On the third night of the meeting about fifty persons asked for prayers, and thirty-four came forward to the altar. An old-fashioned Methodist time was experienced.

The next night witnessed a still greater display of Pentecostal power. The whole audience room was an altar, and in every part of the house persons were seeking for salvation. The christian people of the whole city were being awakened and began to fall in line with the great religious movement that had so auspiciously begun. On Friday evening of the first week, after five nights of earnest work more than one hundred adults had enlisted for Christ, besides scores of children reported in the children's meeting. The evangelists prayed for one hundred more to be converted during the coming Sabbath. On Saturday more ample provisions were made for seating the crowds that were expected on the coming Sabbath. Services were announced to occupy a larger part of the day. An account of the first Sabbath services we clip from one of the Tiffin dailies: "Yesterday was a high day in Zion. At the morning hour a large audience listened to a sermon by the pastor. The prayer service conducted by the evangelist was a season of joy to hundreds of hearts. The children's meeting at four o clock was largely attended. More than a hundred children and youths bowed before God as seekers of pardon and many gave a clear testimony that they had obtained it. At night long before the hour of service the audience room was full of people, and when the services began the house was packed. The parlor and the infant class rooms were filled and many compelled to stand in the aisles."

During the day sixty-nine at children's and young people's meeting professed to have found Christ, and in the evening thirty-four more conversions were reported making more than a hundred in a day for Christ. Mr. Willis was at his best and intensely in earnest, pressing people to immediate decision on the great question of life. The audience was dismissed twice in order that an inquiry meeting might be held, but it was impossible to diminish the crowd enough for this purpose without closing the entire services of the evening. This day of power and Pentecostal display closed the first full week of revival under the the conduct of the evangelists, Mr. and Mrs. Willis, and two hundred converts were claimed as the glad result.

Thus these meetings went on with marked demonstrations and great victory for four weeks. Sometimes the tide of enthusiasm rising higher than others, but with unabated interest throughout, the house being continually crowded at each night's service and sometimes many went away for lack of room. The interest and overflowing house was maintained through bad weather as well as good, through week evenings as well as Sundays.

People went forward to the altar and sought God, and conversions took place by the score, as in the first week of the meetings. Sometimes the christian people were called upon to observe certain days for fasting and prayer; at which time an all-day meeting would be held, when it was in order for persons to engage in the services at will. No abatement of interest or power was observed, but rather intensified.

On the 24th after nearly three weeks of service it was stated that the jam was so great that the workers could with difficulty get through the congregation. The request was twice made for those who were not personally interested to retire; but no one seemed willing to go. On Monday, the 29th of January, the converts had reached the number of four hundred and twenty-four. It was announced that services would continue during the coming week, and on the following Friday evening a praise meeting was held over five hundred that had been converted.

In these wonderful meetings it would not be strange that some interesting and striking incidents should occur worthy of mention, and which if told would illustrate more fully the great work of the Lord, accomplished at the hands of his servants and evangelists. On one evening a christian man who had heard of this great revival work came one hundred miles to enjoy an evening in the meetings and when he had looked in upon the meeting, he was satisfied and went away, saying like the queen of the East, "The half was not told unto me."

An almost opposite effect was had upon two unconverted men who came to the meeting, but as the services progressed they became restless and disquieted and could endure no longer; finally they got up and rushed out of the church, and ran up town and into a barber shop, saying that if there was any such thing as the Holy Ghost they had it down at the Methodist Church, for they had to run or get converted.

Great as were the demonstrations of saving-power, and joyous as were the converts in their experience of the new life, and clear as were the testimonies of full and complete salvation; yet some were asking why there was not the old-time demonstration of power as was experienced fifty years ago, within the recollection of some of the older people. Upon hearing that some had known of greater displays of power than the wonderful experience that they had just witnessed.

Mr. Willis went to his room and fell upon his knees in prayer and did not rise until assured that his eyes should behold something of the old-time power, in displays of saving grace. The next night he arose, called attention to the demonstrations of such meetings, in which men fell prostrate, as dead under the mighty power of God. And stated that he believed that it would be so to-night. And so it proved. That night a strong, able bodied man came to the altar, and had not been there long until he fell over like one dead. They tried to bend his arms, his arm was inflexible, he was pierced with pins by others but he was unmoved as a corpse. Only a little while however did this condition continue when he jumped up with a shout of victory, testifying of the salvation of God he had received. His future testimony and life proved that he was most thoroughly converted.

The same night another man fell back in his seat and his friends thinking that he was dying gathered around him, but Mr. Willis said make room, he is dying for want of Christ. Coming to himself in a little while he motioned for them to make room at the altar, and in a few minutes he was sweetly saved and healed of all his malady of sins. In his testimony he said that he had promised his wife that morning that he would seek God on that night, and should surely have died had he not come to the altar that night. This was a revival also much after the old time. Many other incidents might be given, but the short space of this work will not allow of the multiplication further than to illustrate the character of the scenes and services through which the evangelists were daily passing and the manner in which God used them in the salvation of many souls. As the meeting approached its close on Friday evening, February 2d, a consecration and praise service was held over the five hundred that had been converted in the past few weeks. It proved to be a jubilee of rejoicing over what God had wrought, and joyous testimonies were given until three hundred and ten had witnessed of the grace of God and his saving power. On the same night others went to the altar and found peace in believing. It was now announced that the coming Sabbath would be the last day the evangelists would be present with them in the work in Tiffin. The last service came on Sabbath evening, and before the time of service the house was so packed with the crowd that it was scarcely possible for the evangelists to pass through. The text selected was Phil. 3:14, "I press forward to the mark of the prize, etc." The altar was again filled, and a glorious victory was achieved in the name of the Lord. Thirty entire families and some six hundred souls had come into the Kingdom. The exclamation of the evangelist was "Glory to Jesus, for mighty victory. We still keep marching on. Thanks be to God who giveth us the victory." Truly this is a marvelous work of the Lord.

AFTER THE REVIVAL.

One question of stupendous greatness with almost every church is to have a revival. The next question of interest arising is, will the work last and will substantial results remain after the revival?

In this revival just described the answer reveals the fact that the work was genuine and of a lasting character. Various denominations of the town shared largely in the fruits of the revival and yet one hundred and eighty remained with the Methodist Church on probation, besides a large class of children under twelve years of age who gave good evidence of conversion. After the meetings closed conversions continued and more than a month later the pastor writes the evangelist saying, "Our work here is still full of interest, accessions at every meeting. Eight last Sabbath and four of our most prominent citizens; our prayer-meetings are large enough for Sunday congregations."

The probationers, for the most part, remained steadfast, and a large majority have been received into full connection. The reception day six months later was a notable day; for the church took in more members, it was said, than were ever received at one time by an evangelical church in that part of the country. After the reception it was evident that all departments of the church work had been quickened, and the church had taken on new life. The Sunday-School flourished, weekly prayer-meetings were strengthened and became seasons of great interest. Steps were taken to complete the audience room of the new church building which had been unfinished for ten years, while the congregation worshipped in the basement, and before a year after the revival all was accomplished. The church was finished at a cost of $15,000.00, and on January 16th, a church worth $50,000.00 was dedicated clear of debt, amid the rejoicing of a delighted people.

With these facts before us it is evident that the work of evangelist Willis and wife in connection with the faithful pastor's labors, was of great permanent value to the congregation on whom he served. We thus dwell, at length, upon this meeting that it may illustrate not only the successes and the emotions and the excitement of revival, but to show their abiding character.

From this city Mr. Willis and wife went out with the good wishes and prayers of both pastor and people, commending them to the world. Pastor Reager in a letter of indorsement says: "Both Harry Willis and wife are evangelists properly accredited by the M. E. Church. During the month of January, 1883, they held meetings for me in the Tiffin M. E. Church. In four weeks between five and six hundred were converted and the entire city was awakened to a religious interest. They are excellent young people, worthy of credit anywhere, and devoted to work for the Lord Jesus. I most cheerfully recommend them to the church wherever they may go. May the Holy Ghost continue to use them for the salvation of souls."

From Tiffin they spend a few days with the Methodist Church at Omer, Ohio, in the same county, where they held meetings for a few nights, rescuing some dozen of souls, and from there they go to join in the work at Norwalk, Ohio, with Rev. J. W. Mendenhall, D. D. as pastor. At this place the meeting was, in many respects, like that at Tiffin, only not so long in duration. The house was crowded to its utmost capacity from the beginning. The religious fire began at once to kindle and it was soon evident that a great religious awakening was begun. In a very few nights it is recorded that the altar as well as the front seats were crowded with seekers of salvation. Here, as well as elsewhere, Mr. Willis with the pastor visited during the forenoons, among the people, praying and warning from house to house. In the afternoon meetings were held and sometimes conducted by Mrs. Willis, which became seasons of power. From night to night the wonderful work went on and increased. On the first Sabbath morning nearly all the Sunday-School stood up for the prayers of the church, expressing a desire for personal salvation. The discourse of the pastor in the morning was followed by an altar service, when a number of conversions took place. At 2.30 in the afternoon a meeting for children and young people was held; many came to the altar and twenty-five professed salvation. A praise meeting followed, as had been announced, at 3.00 P. M. over one hundred converts in the past few days and at its close sixty seekers came to the altar and twenty-seven conversions were reported. At night Mr. Willis discoursed on the "Master's Call," and Mrs. Willis exhorted in a most tender and eloquent strain, many going to the altar for the first time. Thus, before the close of the first week of service, the church of Norwalk was in the midst of a gracious revival, and was witnessing the conversion of souls by the score. Already one hundred and thirty-six had professed the saving grace of Jesus.

Among the converts were people of all ages and classes, and varied tastes, opinions and prejudices. The old and the young crowd together at a common altar to crown Jesus Lord of all and receive the salvation of their souls. On one occasion an old lady seventy years of age was found among the seekers at the place of prayer.

On one night the first person at the altar was a man over fifty years of age; about forty others followed. Among the number of converts, on one occasion, was a young lady who had formerly been a member of the Roman

Catholic Church. The discourse on the evening of her conversion was on the final strivings of the Spirit. A mighty power of God rested on the people and many were moved to seek God for the first time. This young lady of fine appearance became so convicted that she took up her book and began to read. In the after meeting Mr. Willis went to speak with her; she only pretended to keep on reading, but soon closed her book and left the room with a haughty air. The evangelist and wife made her a subject of special prayer. At the next afternoon meeting she came again, but on being spoken to on the subject of religion, she left the room as before, but soon after came back and went straight to the altar where she was soon saved and rejoiced with joy unspeakable and full of glory.

As the meeting advanced conversions were continually multiplied. Appointed fast days became days of spiritual feasting, because of the continued outpouring of the spirit and the displays of saving power. They who were willing to show their superior desire for spiritual food above that of the wants of the body feasted on the bread which comes down from heaven.

The seating capacity of the church continued throughout to be too small for the meetings. People stood in the aisles and around about the doors, and many were compelled to go away unable to obtain entrance. The interest deepens and seekers throng the altars even to the close of the meeting, which no doubt would have gone on some days or weeks longer had it not been that the evangelists failed in health and strength necessary to go on with the meeting and must seek much needed rest or be unable for fields of future labor. This they concluded to do and the meeting closed after a series of some two weeks, with something like two hundred converts.

Concerning the evangelists and their work, Dr. Mendenhall, in a note of commendation states : " I take great pleasure in saying that the evangelists, Mr. H. M. Willis and wife spent two weeks with me in christian work in this city. It is not extravagant to say that the result was wonderful. The church was quickened and the unsaved were convicted by the score, and many of them converted. There were fifty-four accessions to the church in two weeks. The evangelists have their own methods, but are not notably eccentric ; and give far less occasion for criticism than others of their class that I know. They are spiritual in their lives, prayerful, earnest and above all the power of God rests upon them. Any church opening its doors to them, and any pastor fully co-operating with them, will find a revival of religion in progress before a week has passed."

Closing at Norwalk they now visit a few days with friends at Republic and Ashland, Ohio, but soon start West on a temporary visit in search of rest and health.

CHAPTER IX.

Seeking Rest and Health.—A few days at Lawrence, Kansas.— Attends Conference at Hiawatha.—Call to State Work.— Returning to Lawrence, Kansas.—Receives many calls to hold Meetings.—Little work undertaken.—Call to Marysville accepted.—The work entered upon.—House overflowing, One Hundred and Sixty Conversions in the meeting.—The church quickened.—Mrs. Willis conducting after services.—Other Churches strengthened. — Extracts from Papers. — People from ten miles away in Attendance.—The Bride and Groom from the Prairie Converted.—Results of the Meeting good.— Testimony of the Pastor.

Leaving Ashland at 7:00 A. M., March 8, 1883, three days after closing the meeting at Norwalk, Mr. Willis and wife started on a visit to the West, hoping to conceal themselves from public attention and find a few weeks or months of quiet rest amid the healthy and invigorating breezes of the western states. Accordingly their baggage was checked for Kansas City, and they were soon on their journey; passing through Toledo, Indiana, Illinois, Missouri, and reaching Kansas City on the following night at 11:30 o'clock. Here they took the train at once for Lawrence, Kansas, and on March 10th registered at the Eldridge House. In this city they located for a few weeks and rented rooms; securing board where they could have rest and quiet quarters for the time they should stay in Lawrence. At this place they met Rev. Wm. Jones, pastor of the Methodist Episcopal Church, of the city, in whom they found a congenial friend, and with him and his estimable family had delightful associations during their stay. They were often invited to his house to dine and enjoy a season of gladness. Being young people themselves Brother and Sister Willis greatly enjoyed the company of Dr. Jones' two children, Nannie and Fred. With them they took walks and carriage rides, and went boating and fishing in the Kansas River, and had many pleasant seasons of recreation.

The next day after their arrival at Lawrence was Sabbath. Instead of the arduous and herculean efforts that had been required of them on many previous Sabbaths, especially at Norwalk and Tiffin, Ohio, in bringing scores and hundreds to Christ, and in assuming responsibility of holding church and people to the great thought of immediate decision, now they had a time of refreshing and a breathing-spell for themselves, nothing to do but to listen to delightful and eloquent sermons from Dr. Jones. Now they could enjoy, like victors, the scenes of the race course or the arena, and for a season could be measurably free from the conflict of the heated strife. Their respite from work being almost a type of that perfect rest when the last battle is fought and we become spectators and are numbered with the crowd of interested witnesses who have kept the faith and won the prize, and now wear the crown.

After a week or more spent in Lawrence, Mr. Willis accompanied Dr. Jones to the Kansas Conference at Hiawatha, where he made pleasant acquaintances with western preachers, and affected some engagements for future work. Here the first day being the examination of classes it was to Mr. Willis, dull business; but in the evening he heard a grand lecture by Dr. Crone, whose subject was: "The Sinner and the Infidel," and with it he was greatly delighted. On the next morning, Bishop Harris presiding, the Conference opened with a communion service which was a most precious and solemn occasion. After this business was taken up and strangers were introduced, and thus Mr. Willis became known to the members of a Western Conference. While at the Conference Mr. Willis received many calls to hold meetings in different places in the State; and among others was an invitation to State work in which he would be a traveling evangelist and under the authority of the church. At this time his mind was still unsettled as to the course to be pursued, and in consequence of the ill health of himself and wife he undertook but little work. He had intended to go to Williamsfield Mineral Springs, and then further west to Colorado; but finding that their health and strength were returning, and that they had found the right place at Lawrence for both rest and health, their stay here was protracted until they felt able to undertake at least some little work in answer to the many calls which were now being made upon them. Among other opportunities a call came from Marysville, Kansas, to hold revival services.

This they concluded to accept, and accordingly on the 7th of April, Brother Willis and wife with many pleasant recollections of the place, leave Lawrence and start for Marysville, a town in the Northern part of Kansas. They go by way of Leavenworth and St. Joseph, stopping at the latter place over Sunday, where they hear Dr. Miller, at Francis Street M. E. Church. On Monday morning they start on their journey, and in the afternoon arrive safely at Marysville, in Marshal County, Kansas, where on the same evening they begin meetings in the M. E. Church, Rev. A. G. Murray, pastor. Here in the West as in the East general religious interest began to be aroused. In a night or two the house was crowded to its utmost capacity; on the second night the altar and three front seats were filled with seekers; and on the third night all but one in the congregation sought either pardon or a clean heart. On the first Sabbath an altar service followed the pastor's morning sermon, and it was blessed with seven conversions.

In the afternoon a praise service was held over the fifty conversions that had been reported to that date. At night the house was crowded within and surrounded without by anxious people, when sixteen came to the altar and ten were converted. Thus the good work of soul-saving went on under the labors of these earnest workers. During the meeting Mrs. Willis often led the afternoon meetings, and sometimes took the night service with powerful effect. In the midst of this great work Mr. Willis had a strong hold on the hand of God and at one place in his journal he states that on one evening before the meeting he went out over the prairies until he came to a place between two bluffs where he prayed for special power, dedicating himself anew, and pleading especially for Marysville: "O God without thy help I am an entire failure Dear Lord give power, give victory and grace to overcome. Help me and my dear wife to cling close to Thee. Amen." Thus he continually maintained his covenant with God and leaned hard on the Divine arm. The people had a mind to work and conversions were multiplied, so that God gave him a splendid victory. The church was quickened and many sinners converted. Other churches also reaped largely from the fruits of this wonderful work of grace.

At this meeting some especially interesting incidents occurred. One is that of the presence of a newly married couple. Rev. Murray during a certain day went out on the prairies some ten miles to unite a couple in marriage. At the wedding the minister spoke of the revival going on, conducted by the evangelist, and invited the company to come and hear them.

Accordingly the bride and groom with a number of their friends were present at the evening service The groom was tall and gaunt while the bride was short and small. They came up the aisle together, she with mouth and eyes open holding his hand. The house was crowded and in the absence of ushers, and to relieve their evident embarrassment, Mr. Willis seeing their dilemma made room for them on a front seat. The pastor whispered that they were the bride and groom of the day. They paid close attention to the sermon, and when through preaching Mr. Willis went to the man and asked him if he would not like to be present at the marriage supper of the Lamb. The case was clear and together they kneeled at the altar of prayer where they dedicated themselves to God and were both converted, "receiving the end of their faith, even the salvation of their souls." How wise at the last was their course at this meeting!

Another interesting conversion in this meeting was that of a man who had held a place on the staff of one of the leading New York Dailies, but who drifted out West and became a great gambler and "confidence man." One morning he came into the Sabbath School Salvation service where Mr. Willis talked with him. He became so interested that he attended the praise services in the afternoon, and in the testimony meeting his heart was so touched that he asked Mr. Willis to pray for him. He was weary and heavy laden with his weight of sin and woe and could wait no longer. He must be saved now or lost forever. He cast himself on the mighty Savior and found peace and pardon and the joy of this great Salvation.

This meeting and religious interest attracted people for many miles around. The testimony of pastor Murray bears witness to the good effects of these special services. One of the Marysville papers in speaking of this meeting conducted by Mr. and Mrs. Willis, at the time, said: "This is undoubtedly the greatest revival that ever visited this part of the State. All churches are being strengthened, about fifty have united with the Methodist Church, quite a number have gone to the Presbyterian and some to the Baptist Church. The number of converts at this time is about one hundred and sixty. The number of seekers was nearly twenty last night."

Thus God was with his chosen workers in the West, and day by day owned the labor of their hands; and Marysville was flooded with a tidal wave of salvation.

CHAPTER X.

Abilene, Kansas.—On way, discovered by a Pastor.—An unprecedented Eulogy.—Invited to tarry and hold a Revival Service, but was engaged for Abilene.—On account of his Wife's Health could undertake no more work.—Successful work and some remarkable incidents.—Formalism receives a hard blow.—Church membership without Salvation.—A Rich Experience and a Grand Testimony.

Going to the West Mr. and Mrs. Willis thought to spend some time as a sort of vacation, but in a few weeks were induced to undertake a meeting or two only. And, now having completed their work undertaken at Marysville they engaged for a like service with the M. E. Church at Abilene, in Dickenson County, Central Kansas, Rev. E. W. VanDeventer, pastor. On the route to Abilene from Marysville an interesting episode occurred at a town where they were to change cars and were compelled to stop for a few hours. A Methodist Church stood just opposite to the hotel where they had stopped. It was prayer-meeting evening, a good number were going. Mr. Willis and wife, as was their custom, always worshipped as they had opportunity. They supposed that they were total strangers to all, in such a distant and strange land; but on entering the house and going quietly to a seat the minister arose and without apparently having noticed the strangers, spoke as follows: "Friends: there is in the house to-night a young man, one of the greatest evangelists of the age, who started as a young boy in Ohio to work for God. His methods are peculiar, but he has the power of the Holy Ghost upon him, and hence thousands of souls are brought to Christ by his labors. That young man is the " Boy Evangelist " of Ohio. Pointing to Mr. Willis, he said: "There he is."

On this extraordinary and unlooked for introduction at a place where he thought he was completely hid, Mr. Willis came forward and talked awhile and prayed, and thus contributed to the interest of the meeting. Before leaving the church he was strongly solicited to tarry and hold a revival meeting in the place; but being engaged for Abilene, and Mrs. Willis' health being yet very feeble, he could make no more arrangements in the West for the present. They bade good-bye to their newly formed friends and took the first train for Abilene, where they arrived with safety in due time. Information concerning this meeting as to numbers and facts is difficult to obtain. The pastor had announced in suitable terms, their coming, through the pulpit and weekly press. It was stated that H. M. Willis and wife from

Ohio would hold a series of Gospel meetings in the M. E. Church at Abilene, commencing May 10, 1883, at 7:30 P. M., and that thousands of souls had been converted under their labors. A week later one of the Abilene papers stated that "Rev. Willis, the Evangelist, is holding a successful revival meeting at the M. E. Church. The interest increases as the meeting progresses." At the end of five days' services, in a letter to his father, Mr. Willis states that about fifty have been converted, and exclaims " Praise God."

The meetings continued some weeks and as a result, which invariably attended the meetings of these evangelists, a great awakening took place. The church was signally stirred out of its formalism, and all classes were reached. One instance of reaching and saving persons from among the refined classes of society in this place is especially interesting. It was that of the wife of Dr. Meredith, who was in Abilene at the time of the meeting. She was a lady of much refinement and great popularity in the place, a member of the Presbyterian Church, but very formal in all her religious exercises, " having the form but denying the power of Godliness," attending fashionable balls and operas and enjoying card-playing like a great many other professed christians. On the first Sabbath Mr. Willis preached from the subject, "Are you saved." Mrs. Meredith and also her husband, the Doctor, were so wrought upon, that upon invitation for seekers they were the first at the altar. They were saved by the power of the truth, and launched out into a rich experience in Christ. In her testimony afterwards Mrs. Meredith said: "When Mr. Willis repeated those words again and again, 'Are you saved?' they fell with such force that I trembled, and my heart said what shall I do? Eternity is before me, and though I am a church-member I am not saved. I was in haste to go to the altar and I am glad I went."

This wonderful conversion created no small stir in the place, for on the following day it was noised all over the city that Mrs. Meredith was at the altar, and the answer came back; "No, not the elegant Mrs. Meredith." But it was true; and the lady of refinement and of formal piety was reached and lifted up into a realm of experience in Christ to which she was ever before an entire stranger. In this instance and in others, formalism, and church-membership without a religious experience received a hard blow, and here many witnesses were raised up in favor of the simple faith of the gospel with the power to melt the heart and change the conduct and make the life sublimely beautiful in Christ.

Closing the meeting at Abilene with much success and many souls saved, and after about three weeks of service, Mr. Willis and wife are again free to spend the remainder of the Summer where they may think best. Not desiring to take up further work at present in the West, and having spent some three months in Kansas, partly in recreation and partly in work, and with greatly improved health and strength by their stay in the West, they now, in the month of June, decide upon a return to Ohio; and accordingly bade good-bye to western scenes and cities to look upon them no more. Their steps are now Eastward bound and soon again they reach their own state, Ohio, improved in health, richer in experience and bearing many pleasant recollections of their Western work and trip.

Eternity alone will reveal all the significance of this visit of the evangelist beyond the Mississippi, and the garnered sheaves of eternity alone will number its spiritual results and tell of all the good accomplished.

CHAPTER XI.

Returning to the East.—Rents a Furnished Cottage in Republic, Ohio, in June, intending to Rest for the Summer.—Brother Guard invites him to Melmore in July.—He can not be hid. —The Cry of Souls is heard.—Holds a two weeks' Meeting at Melmore.—A wonderful Revival in Harvest Time.—More than one hundred Conversions.—NEVADA.—Called by the Presiding Elder to fill the Pulpit at Nevada.—Traveling a Circuit till Conference, as a Supply.—He preaches in the Street.—The White Horse.—Crowds hear him from his Carriage Pulpit.—Delivers up his Charge at Conference.— Visits other Conferences.

Returning from Abilene, Kansas, Mr. Willis and wife now seek a temporary location in their own State, where they may spend the Summer and the heated season among friends and old acquaintances. Accordingly, Republic, an interesting village in Seneca County, is selected. Here Rev. C. E. Ruddick, father of Mrs. Willis, pastor of the Methodist Episcopal Church, resided, and of course, this fact heightened the attractiveness of the place to them as a temporary home. They here rent a furnished cottage and set up cosily for themselves, expecting a pleasant season of Summer vacation and home-like life together.

But soon Brother Guard of the Melmore Charge, North Ohio Conference, finds his quiet retreat, and although it is now near the middle of June, yet he invites Brother Willis to hold a revival meeting in the M. E. Church at Melmore, Ohio, at once assuring him that the urgency was so great that his services were greatly needed in that place in the interest of perishing souls. Mr. Willis considered this pressing call as the voice of the Lord. And although it was contrary to his arranged plans for the Summer, yet God's directions and call to him were always supreme and imperative. He could not be hid and he would not turn away from the call of Providence. The cry of souls was heard. Mr. Willis, leaving his wife in her quiet home in company with a sister, was soon on the ground ready for the work of soul-saving at Melmore. The meeting at once began and the work went on with vigor and great success. In less than a week the place was shaken under the power of God. The current of iniquity was checked and the course of vice was arrested. Satan's kingdom was molested and souls were plucked as brands from the burning. Opposition and strong threats were made from without against the evangelist, but he was fearless, for he rested under the protection of the Almighty; and at one time when opposition was the fiercest, God raised him up a band of strong protectors, who guarded his body from the fury of those, who had been disturbed by his bold attack upon sin and iniquity of every description. The meeting went on to its consummation, foes subsided and a hundred souls in a little village of less than one thousand inhabitants, were rescued and converted to God. Thus in a fortnight, about the beginning of harvest time, God wrought at the hand of his servant, and a mighty awakening took place at a time, when by tacit consent the Church generally reposes, or at least does nothing more than to "hold the fort" and wait for the coming good time of late Fall or early Winter All times and seasons are alike with God, and when man is ready for the harvest, God is willing to work by many or by few. Too often there is the long and tedious waiting when all that is needed is to rise up at God's call and go forth to speedy victory.

From this field of victory Mr. Willis, though not a preacher in the authorized sense of the word, but simply a lay-worker and evangelist, was invited by the Presiding Elder to take charge of a circuit for a short time, until Conference would convene. Not desiring to travel in the heated season as an evangelist, he accepted the invitation of Presiding Elder A. Polock, and was accordingly appointed to succeed Rev. C. W. Crawford and take charge of Nevada Circuit for the remainder of the Conference year. Early in July, 1883, Mr. Willis entered upon the discharge of his duties as preacher in charge of the circuit, and commenced preaching regularly on Sabbaths at the various appointments. It was somewhat of a novelty for him to engage in a work of this kind. He would now have the oversight of the church, as well as the work of an evangelist. With the reputation which he had now acquired, his presence on the charge created no small stir and curiosity. They looked upon him as one of the most successful evangelists in the Church—a second Harrison.

His regular appointment on the circuit became a season of much interest and many people heard him gladly. Not confining himself to the Church edifice he sometimes extended his influence and enlarged his congregation by singing and preaching on the streets. Sometimes he would drive to the place with a white horse and carriage and from the carriage in the street, deliver the message of truth. A clipping from the *Nevada Enterprise* of August 10, '83, states that " On last Sabbath evening the ' Boy Evangelist' held a very interesting service on Main street in front of the Bank Block, where he was greeted by a large and appreciative audience. He will hold services on next Sunday evening at seven o'clock. Whether in the pastorate or in the field as evangelist he was an inveterate worker. On one Sabbath his announcements of services were as follows: At M. E. Church, at Nevada, preaching at 10:30 o'clock A. M.; at the Burke Church, at 2:30 P. M.; at Wyandot at 4:30 P. M., also street services at Nevada at 7:30 P. M."

Thus fulfilling faithfully and acceptably the duties of his work for the time appointed, he delivered up his charge at the session of Conference in September, and was again ready for the field as an evangelist. Attending the Central Ohio Conference, and, also the North Ohio Conference, in which he had served as a supply preacher, he received numerous invitations to go out again in the campaign of soul-saving among the Churches of Ohio.

Ever since his entrance into the evangelistic work it was never difficult for him to obtain a field of labor; but the main question of importance to decide was, which door to enter. In fact, sometimes as high as three hundred invitations for evangelistic work were before him at one time. It is marvelous to comtemplate, but such was the desire for revivals, that a great cry arose for the services of the evangelists.

Often their presence alone would inspire great faith and seem sufficient to produce the desired results. Here was a workman who never entered a field of revival effort without glorious and abundant results, and one whose services as such met with increasing demand.

CHAPTER XII.

Invitations received.—Wonderful cry for Evangelist.—He accepts Hicksville.—The Correspondence.—The Situation.—Hard Pounding both Ways.—Holding on by Faith.—In Darkness. —Soon the Heavens are Light—The Great victory.—The Holy Ghost fell on all—The Melting Time—The great Deep broken up.—Sinners crying and Converts shouting.— An Editor saved.—A Time of great Rejoicing.—The Beginning of great Prosperity.—CAREY, OHIO.—The Altar filled.—The Cry of Agony.—Salvation comes.—The Crowds too great.—An old Man taking Christ on Testimony and is saved.—Numbers added to both Churches.—Pastor Taneyhill. —UPPER SANDUSKY.—A Two Weeks Engagement. —Brother D. Cook, pastor.—Three Score of Substantial Converts.—God owns His Workmen and the Work moves on.

Among the numerous invitations which Mr. Willis received to hold revival services, was one from the pastor and people of Hicksville M. E. Church, Defiance County, Ohio, Rev. Joseph D. Simms, pastor. This is a growing town of some two thousand inhabitants, situated on the line of the B. & O. R. R., two miles east of the Indiana State line. The Methodists of this place in former years worshipped in the Presbyterian church, and not until within about seven years of the time of which we are about to write did they have a Church of their own. They then built a beautiful church costing about $6,000. No great revival had been enjoyed since the formation of the class, but the accessions and increase were by gradual growth and largely from Methodists moving to the place and finding a home in their own Church. Years of early association and worship with Presbyterians was of an educating character, in the line of Church usages and proprieties, but was not conducive to the old-fashioned Methodist revival spirit. After the erection of their own house of worship Methodist usages and customs had more freedom and better opportunities for observance. They now began to hold services uninfluenced by the methods of any other denomination. Revival meetings were held almost annually under various pastors with some good results and generally with some few accessions; but the spirit of power did not rest mightily on the Church, but rather a nice propriety and formal state of religious feeling prevailed. Numerically the Church had increased and strengthened each year, and a deepening of the religious life and a desire for spiritual things gradually became more and more apparent. The need of a genuine and thorough revival was earnestly felt and the assurance that such would soon be enjoyed was a growing conviction. This conviction was so strong that one man remarked that "the next time we hold a meeting here we must go in for a grand success."

The charge now numbered about one hundred substantial members, and the society had been raised from a circuit to the rank of a station, with preaching both morning and evening. On the return of the pastor for the third year in the Fall of 1883, it was manifest that, with the good feeling among the membership and the deep religious interest prevailing and especially with a strong desire to see souls saved, this was the opportune time for a revival meeting. The pastor realized that for this work a little foreign help of a proper character would add inspiration and enthusiasm to the movement and might greatly facilitate the work. Accordingly on a Sabbath, soon after his return from Conference, he made known to the congregation his own heart-felt desire to see the work of the Lord revived in the place, and that to this end he felt that a little help in holding Gospel services would greatly aid the work; and more than this the providence of God had thrown in his way the opportunity of securing the help of two distinguished workers, husband and wife, whose presence had been attended everywhere they went with glorious results. The Church at once authorized an arrangement with these workers, and accordingly, H. M. Willis and wife were engaged to assist the pastor in conducting a meeting in the M. E. Church of Hicksville, to commence October 20, 1883.

The correspondence between the pastor and Brother Willis brought out some suggestions concerning the preliminary work as well as the expression of the hope by Mr. Willis for a successful revival. He desired that meetings should begin at least a week before his coming. Among the suggestions for the conduct of services before his arrival, was that there should be a "Great deal of praying; can do nothing without the Holy Spirit's guidance and power; must be an expectancy and faith on the part of the people; get the faith of the people to a good point; everybody to praying; ask God and believe Him; hold on to God for victory; nothing impossible with Him; let us lie very low at the foot of the cross and proclaim victory in the name of the Lord."

With these suggestions and a preliminary meeting of one week's duration, which elicited some interest and enlisted prayer for victory, the way was in some degree prepared; yet the great deep was by do means broken up. "Much land yet remained to be possessed," and much hard work yet remained to bring the church in line with radical revival work. Mr. Willis and wife arrived Saturday, October 20th. On Sabbath morning after a discourse from the pastor, Brother Willis gave a few words of exhortation, and prophesy, stating that a revival was just at hand. A like faith, on solicitation, was also expressed on the part of the church. In the evening the evangelist had charge of the services and preached in his own peculiar style and manner, which at once seemed odd, nervous and eccentric, and appeared to some to violate all rules of order and propriety. The house was well filled but some went away dissatisfied saying, they would never hear him again. Nothing signal occurred that evening only that a new form of evangelism had appeared and a bold and sturdy movement was inaugurated, such that the members and people would hardly endure, many standing aloof to see what would become of it. The next night revealed that some had stayed away, thinking that they would take no part. To the surprise of Mr. Willis the congregation was less than on the Sunday evening before, and on coming to the house late and finding the congregation smaller, he exclaimed: "It will take three nights at this rate to get an audience," although the house was then well filled. The battle was not to be won without an awful struggle. Each night the meetings went on during the first week without signal results, further than that the audience increased and crowds began to come from near and far, and that a few souls were blessed at each service with salvation. Some were drawn to the work and some were drawn away in opposition. From the journal of Mrs. Willis we quote: "October 20, 1883, we came to Hicksville. Found the church desiring revival services, but when God began to work many of them turned a cold shoulder to us, not liking Mr. Willis' methods, and doing all they could to stop the progress of the revival. The first day we came, the spirit of prayer rested on Mr. Willis and myself. We cried mightily unto God, for we felt that the sin of the people was very great, but we knew nothing of the struggle which we were to pass through, nor the wrestling in prayer, nor the great battle with the powers of darkness we should have e're victory would be on God's side. We began on Sabbath evening, and up to Friday following everything looked very dark, only eight conversions being recorded. And when Mr. Willis dismissed the congregation without the benediction, but cried out in great agony of soul: "Go, go, go,—go home and pray!" consternation fell on the people, many of the church members became much insulted, and some even wanted to close the church door against us; but the pastor, Rev. J. D. Simms, a man of faith and prayer stood nobly by us. Never flinching, holding up our hands, praying God to give us the victory. Mr. Willis went to the parsonage refusing to see any one's face until Sunday, except those of the family, and after spending much time in tears, groans and prayers, his face suddenly lighted up with the glory of God, and he shouted "Glory! glory!! glory!!! The next day (Saturday) the clouds gathered darker and darker. Satan seemed to be let loose; but we continued much in prayer. About six o'clock, the time of evening prayers, the door-bell rang and a man tremblingly handed Brother Simms a note for Mr. Willis which contained words of sweet cheer. The writer of the note begged Mr. Willis to be of good cheer, as many prayers were going up at that hour for him and for the conversion of Hicksville. This note came from a man of position and influence."

From this brief sketch, the situation, at the beginning, of the meeting, and at the end of the first week may be clearly seen. The next day was the second Sabbath of the meeting. The superintendent, R. F. Kerr, a man of God and deeply interested in the Spiritual interest of the young, had arrived on Saturday from a business trip in the East and was now present in the Sunday School. He was impressed when away that he ought to hasten so as to be present in the work on the Sabbath and future meetings. His presence was a great help and inspiration in the work. At the morning hour the pastor preached from the text: "Who is on the Lord's side?" and Mrs. Willis followed with a short talk on the subject: " Be filled with the Holy Ghost." The scene which followed was beyond description, in the wonderful display of divine power. God had certainly come suddenly to his temple in the outpouring of his Spirit, so that great and marvelous power came upon the believers. The luke-warm and formal cried out in agony for forgiveness, because they had lived at such a poor dying rate. Sinners fell upon their knees in all parts of the house seeking salvation. And " Heaven came down our souls to greet, while Glory crowned the mercy seat." The meeting lasted and could not be discontinued until one o'clock in the afternoon. The church had humbled herself before the mighty hand of God, and received the enduement of power for the first time in her history, and now the glory of the Lord had risen upon her. The joy of the Lord was her strength, and sinners felt that the time had come for them to repent and be converted, that their sins might be blotted out. From this time forward, during all the meeting which lasted for some three weeks longer, victory was on Israel's side, and seekers by the score thronged the altar and rejoiced in the salvation of our God. The Church hungered and thirsted after righteousness and were filled. A holy desire and burden of soul rested on the Christian worker, and parents longed and labored for the salvation of their children. One woman so earnestly sought the conversion of her only boy that she prayed constantly and declared her purpose to fast until her son should be saved. That evening amidst the throng of people, and with the tide of seekers he pressed his way to the altar and soon rejoiced in the pardon of sin and the hope of heaven. The people of various classes were seized with a constraining desire to be saved, and men who had at the beginning of the meeting made all manner of fun and indulged in hard sayings were afterwards among the suppliants for mercy and salvation, and engaged enthusiastically in the promotion of the work.

As the revival went on many clear and beautiful conversions were witnessed, but none more signal and beautiful than that of M. L. Starr, then one of the editors of the Hicksville *News*, a young man of good character, with rare abilities and good worldly prospects. He had been a member of the Sunday School and was interested somewhat in the Church of which his pious mother was a member. Among the first seekers, after the Church had gotten in line of work, was young Starr. It was on the second Sunday evening of the meeting, October 28th. The house was crowded and many compelled to stand. The altar was being filled with earnest seekers. His opportunity of a lifetime was at hand. Duty was clear—he ought to be a Christian and commence now. With manly courage he left the crowd among whom he was standing, in the rear of the church, and walking the whole length of the long aisle he bowed at the altar of prayer before the God of heaven, and under a deep sense of need and of the just claims of God in Christ, he consented to be saved, and within ten minutes arose with a countenance radiant with joy, and in expressions of delight he testified of the great and wonderful salvation of Christ. He afterwards said that he wanted to seek God early in the meeting so as to commence duty soon, and be free quickly, free from all his sins so as to enjoy more of the meeting with the people of God. His life afterwards showed the reality of the work in his heart, and while he remained in Hicksville he was President of the young people's Religious Society, and greatly aided in the work of the Master. On removal to Goshen, Indiana, where he became one of the editors of the *Goshen Daily Independent*, he took a church certificate, and was there greeted by the Church and was given abundant Christian work to do, which he willingly accepted in Christ's name. Many other interesting conversions might be cited, would the limits of our space allow or the design of the book demand it.

The meeting under the lead of evangelist Willis went on here, in all, for some four weeks, until more than one hundred had professed Christ. Victory came abundantly until it was a complete triumph. Though it was through the severest conflict yet the Lord's cause triumphed gloriously. The struggle was fierce and hard, and once after the meeting was fairly progressing, and on account of the intrepid boldness and keen and cutting charges upon the enemy, Mr. Willis even received blows from an unconverted sinner, who, one evening after the meeting, came to the very railing of the church and struck down the evangelist, who, on recovering, only replied that it was "A cowardly act to strike a man when off his guard." In a day or two under good medical care Mr. Willis was again in the meeting, with a sweet spirit working as hard and fearlessly as ever for Christ, no interruption in the spiritual results or progress of the meeting having taken place, but rather the Lord turned " the wrath of man to praise him," and many souls came to Christ.

This meeting will be looked back upon as an epoch of great interest in the history of Hicksville Methodism, and will mark the beginning of greater spiritual prosperity, as well as to have strengthened the things which were weak, in a more material way. From this year the Society became a full station, dropping the country appointment and rising to the rank of one of the best charges, and afterwards enjoying the services of some of the best preachers of the Conference.

This Church will doubtless rejoice for time to come over the work done and the souls saved in this wonderful meeting in the Fall of 1883.

After Hicksville, through the earnest request of Pastor Taneyhill, and the M. E. Church, evangelist Willis and wife next engaged in revival meetings at Carey, Ohio, a beautiful town of 1500 inhabitants on the line of I. B. & W. R. R., at its junction with the C. H. V. & T. R. R., in Wyandot County. At this meeting, crowds soon overflowed the audience room of the church so that as early as five o'clock standing room was scarcely to be obtained. Doors were locked at an early hour to prevent a jam and allow room for workers. The altar was soon thronged with prostrate seekers and many young and old men were moved to seek God in the salvation of their souls. I need not write of this meeting in detail, suffice it to quote a few words from the *Western Christian Advocate* in the report of the meeting which was made on December 26, 1883, and close with a few words from Rev. C. W. Taneyhill, who was then serving his third year as pastor of the station. The *Western Christian Advocate* of the date mentioned said: "At Carey, Ohio, the revival has been a great blessing and success under the leadership of Brother and Sister H. M. Willis, evangelists. In the couple of weeks that they were there, nearly one hundred were converted, some of them having been in the Church for years."

At the close of the meetings, December, 1883, Pastor Taneyhill, in a note of commendation, speaks the following kind words: "Brother and Sister H. M. Willis having shown full proof of their calling as evangelists of the Lord Jesus, whose they are in body and spirit, proven by works and faith, having held a meeting at Carey, Central Ohio Conference, I can not but give voluntarily this feeble attestation. By stirring up the lukewarm, quickening the careless, by the conversion of unbelievers, by the purifying of the saved, full proof of power with God and man was shown. By faith, mountains of difficulty were removed; by faith, prejudice gave way to love; by faith, the Church society stands united as never before."

On hearing afterwards of the death of Brother Willis, as late as October 25, 1885, Pastor Taneyhill took occasion to write to Sister Willis a few lines which express further information concerning the work of this meeting and the high esteem in which Brother Willis and his faithful companion were held. This letter dated from Bowling Green, Ohio, October 22, 1885, says: "Brother Willis and wife were with me at Carey, Ohio, Central Ohio Conference. Many are the souls that rejoice in the prospect of a better world through the work done at that time. The zeal of the Master's cause, the saving of souls while it made life more glorious, also spent the oil much sooner. Unswerving faith would mount upward above obstacles as the eagle above the clouds, while it would bask in the eternal sunlight of God's love. A very old man said only a few days ago, 'I am so glad the invitation was given me that night and I came to Christ my Savior.' The prayers of the church at Carey often ascended on the Thursday night prayer meetings for Brother and Sister Willis as they went to Africa. Most of us thinking it would not be long for them but even this was sooner than we expected, the coming of the Master. Long will the halo of glory enshrine the pure life influences of Brother Willis, and long may the sustaining grace be given in copious showers to sustain Sister Willis in the darksome days of widowhood."

From Carey, Brother and Sister Willis were invited to Upper Sandusky to hold a meeting at the M. E. Church of which Rev. D. R. Cook was pastor. This city is but eleven miles distant from Carey, the scene of their last labors, and at which meeting the Rev. Cook and wife were often present helping in the services and becoming thoroughly acquainted with the manner and methods of the evangelist. Without rest or delay they entered upon the work at Upper Sandusky. Of this meeting (after it had been in progress only a little more than a week) Mr. Willis in a letter to the writer said, " We are having a good time. Every day souls are saved. Up to date Brother Cook reports sixty-two clear conversions. One young man was unable to get to the altar but fell in the aisle, flat on his face, before he got within four or five seats of it. Great excitement prevails, bibles are being searched in houses and stores, barber-shops, saloons and everywhere. Deep conviction has fallen upon the town. The Devil is mad. Threats are being made. We have been warned against ringing the church-bell. O, how I wish you were here to enjoy the glorious refreshing. It is an old time revival. All praise to the Trinity, Hallelujah to the Lamb."

From one of the local papers of Upper Sandusky we clip the following report of the work and the workers: " Mr. and Mrs. Willis, the evangelists, who have been conducting revival meetings in the M. E. Church for the past three weeks left here last Saturday for Ashland, where Mr. Willis' parents reside, to take a short rest from their spiritual labors. Their efforts here were crowned with success, and during their stay they made many warm friends, who were loath to see them depart."

Farther than this it is unnecessary to speak. The workers labored hard enjoying the co-operation of pastor and people, great good was accomplished and more than half a hundred were added to the Church. The evangelists departed, leaving behind them many new converts, and a strengthened Church, and bearing away with them the prayers and well-wishes of those with whom they labored.

CHAPTER XIII.

LIMA, OHIO.—Pastor Davies in charge of a great Church invites Evangelist Willis.—Much work ahead.—Hard Fighting.—The awakening Spirit on the City.—Crowds attend.— Scores are Converted.—One hundred and thirty-six decide for Christ.—FOSTORIA, OHIO.—Jonathan and his Armor-bearer.—The Church at ease.—The Few —The Pastor and Evangelist.—Earnest Work —Pulling out of the Fire, one hundred and twenty-five plucked as Brands.—The Church greatly revived.

From upper Sandusky, after a short rest with friends and relatives, according to previous arrangement, the evangelists proceeded to Lima, Ohio. Here they enter upon work in the Trinity M. E. Church, which is one of the largest and costliest church edifices in Ohio.

Of this church the Rev. J. F. Davies was at that time the pastor. His congregation was always large and his people enthusiastic in church enterprises, and in various forms of church work. But no great revival had been enjoyed for several years. Pastor Davies desiring to see the salvation of many souls before the expiration of his three years pastorate, which was just closing, concluded to call to his aid the young and noted evangelists, H. M. Willis and wife, who were at that time available for his charge, and might be yoked for the load, or hitched on as a tug to get the great vessel out of the harbor, to have better chance for the favorable breezes. It will not be our purpose to give an extended account of this meeting, or in any wise to enter into detail with reference to the varied and various features of the work; but may say, that here as everywhere, there were great difficulties to meet and overcome. The cold and back-slided, and the unconverted in the church were not ready for radical old-fashioned and high-pressure revival movements, and they hindered the work. The wise, formal and proper looked upon the methods of the evangelists as too irregular and eccentric, and without a due regard for the proprieties of such a refined presence, and so they opposed the movement. Nevertheless, the Lord wrought mightily with his servants, the evangelists, and the common people heard them gladly. The house was soon crowded to its utmost capacity. Earnest workers took up the cause. The church became stirred up to healthy action. The awakening Spirit was on the city. The interest increased from day to day until soon more than a score of penitents were forward at the altar at one time, seeking salvation. With much fasting and prayer these earnest workers lead on the services of the revival, until here as elsewhere, many were won to the Kingdom of our Lord, and at least one hundred and thirty-six were converted and dedicated themselves to Christ. God again owned his servants and gave them here continued tokens of divine favor. A refreshing wave of salvation came upon the church and people; and the evangelists retired under the blessing of God to win other souls to Christ.

After the engagement at Lima, the way opened at Fostoria and Rev. Richard Wallace invited the evangelist to join him in a ten-day's meeting, in the M. E. Church, of which he was the pastor. Accordingly early in March, 1884, Mr. Willis strongly supported by the pastor who is himself a most successful revivalist, began a meeting. For several days he was without the aid of Mrs. Willis, who was resting for a short time at Hicksville. Here the usual crowds attended upon the services and hundreds could not get into the church. Early in the meeting in a letter Mr. Willis said: " Last night forty were at the altar, and twenty-four were converted. The church is ever so cold and dead. I told them to stay at home, and many of them did, for they were mad. I expect a full house this morning. The altar will not hold the penitents. Some of the worst in town have been converted. Men leave work and everything to come and seek the Lord. It is wonderful."

Later in writing to his parents, Mr. Willis says: "Up to last night one hundred have been converted and one hundred and twenty-six have been to the altar, within three days. We have a great deal to contend with and have been very sorely tried."

Concerning the evangelist and the work in Fostoria, in a letter to the writer, bearing date November 5, 1885, Pastor Wallace says a few words which may be of interest and value in this place. He said: " Brother Willis held a meeting for me in Fostoria for ten days, and it was quite successful. There were about fifty united with the church on probation, most of whom were taken into full connection. They were nearly all young people. There was not much opposition to him there. Mr. Willis said many things that seemed out of place but he meant it all for the best. I believe he was a good man at heart — a thorough christian. The opposition in Fostoria came from the editors of the papers and the young men outside of the church, but the meeting did the church good. I have often heard him in secret devotion from my study, and more earnest prayer I never heard. He went with me to several places to call on the sick and I never heard his equal in my life in prayer for the sick, and his prayers all came from the heart. There was a tenderness and sympathy about them that would melt the hardest heart. Upon the whole I loved him dearly. He was a christian and I believe is now in heaven."

Having toiled earnestly at Fostoria for ten days or a little more the meeting closed in good order leaving the church increased in numbers and strength. Mr. Willis departed carrying with him the good wishes of the pastor and many kind friends from Fostoria. Mr. Willis held one more meeting in the campaign. The

Spring of the year was passing and Summer would soon be at hand. The Fall and Winter, devoted almost without respite to constant revival work, had told upon the strength and health of both Mr. Willis and wife, who in addition to the exciting and arduous work of the continuous revivals have had the care of their child, who is yet but a small babe less than a year old, and who has been with them in all the vicissitudes and changes of their late itinerating evangelistic tours. They must soon halt and rest for a season or the life of both, parents and child, will be endangered. Many fields are yet open and opportunities for service are abundant. They can undertake but little more work of the kind for the season, but concluded to hold one more short meeting, and accordingly accept an invitation from the M. E. Church at Stryker, Ohio, a small town on the east edge of Williams County. Here Rev. N. S. Brackney was the pastor. The evangelists could remain and work but a few days. The battle must be pressed to the gate. The law and gospel are proclaimed with great plainness of speech. Motives for immediate action are presented from every source; heaven is portrayed; the certainty of death and uncertainty of life; and especially were the awful realities of hell unfolded. The power of song was brought to bear. The people were attracted. The fire was kindled and began to glow, to

> "Burn up the dross of base desire
> And make the mountains flow!"

The Universalists, of whom there is a good number in this community, were displeased, but the Church was being benefitted and many were rejoicing in the good work, which was set in motion almost as by magic. One service in these meetings was spoken of as a "general forgiveness asking time" in the Church, when long estranged hands were clasped in friendship. Tomahawks were buried with resolutions to forgive and forget old difficulties and live more in accord with the golden rule of truth and love. At another service eighteen penitents were at the altar, desiring the prayers and sympathies of the Church in their efforts to come to Christ for salvation. In the eight evenings that this meeting was held a glorious work was accomplished and many were saved through the earnest labors of evangelist Willis and wife. Their work, under God, at this place will long be remembered, and the workers will be held in highest esteem.

With this meeting the evangelistic labors of H. M. Willis and wife closed for the season, and as it afterwards appeared, this was the last meeting that they ever held in Ohio. Their work together in the West was finished forever. They now, late in the Spring of 1884, retired from public life for the Summer, and sought a rest in private life at Tiffin, Ohio. Here Mr. Willis engaged in business for a brief season, as a temporary change and rest from the severe nervous strain of revival work. Here their child grew stronger, and Mrs. Willis recruited her health. It was altogether only another season of preparation, or reparation, where God teaches and prepares them for still greater trials and victories of faith, which were yet to come, and which the Lord was holding in reserve for them. The future was unknown but they trusted God day by day, and awaited his divine direction in all things.

CHAPTER XIV.

PHILADELPHIA, PA., October, 1884.—Again in the Field.—A Call to be assistant Pastor in the City, Salary offered.—Opening Prospects.—Accepts Evangelistic Work in West Philadelphia, with Rev. Clark, Pastor.— A Good Meeting.— NORRIS SQUARE.—Providential Opening.—Rev. Thos. Harrison, Pastor.—Evangelist Willis invited.—First night fifty-three at the Altar.—Signal Victory.—The Good Work continues.—More than two hundred Converted.—Another Account.—The Work and Workers Appreciated.—The Last Revival of Brother Willis.

In October, 1884, Mr. Willis was again in the field ready for duty wherever the Lord would call. His mind was now directed to the East. He visited Philadelphia, Pa. Here he mingled among the Christian people and made observations as to the opportunities for Christian work in the city. He did not wait long. God was directing all his steps and leading his servant in a plain path. Calls in this new field began to be made and the way at once opened. One day while attending a service of the Y. M. C. A., of which he had long been a member, a stranger came to him and asked him to visit Rev. Wm. Taylor, pastor of the First Reformed Church of the city. The object was an interview with Mr. Willis to see if his services could be secured as assistant pastor, to do the city missionary work of the First Reformed Church, one of the largest and wealthiest churches of the city. The consistory unanimously decided to secure his services if possible, and made an offer of a liberal salary with the promise that if the work demanded it they would build him a tabernacle for evangelistic work. This offer Mr. Willis at first was inclined to accept, and sent for his wife who was yet in Ohio to come, that with her concurrence he might accept and make more thorough arrangements for the work. But this plan was not to be carried out. God had abundant work for Mr. Willis in the church of his choice and in the line of his special adaptation, where he could exercise the utmost freedom in his own peculiar methods and win victories for the Lord, in a wider sphere than could be won within the limits of any one local church.

Instead of accepting the offer, thus presenting itself, the way of the Lord appeared clearer in another direction. A call came from a church in West Philadelphia, of which the Rev. N. W. Clark was pastor. This they concluded to accept, and were soon engaged in the work among the people of their own loved Methodism. Here as elsewhere the blessing of the Lord attended their labors, and another glorious work was soon in progress, and a goodly number of conversions were reported. The writer not having the data or details of the work of this place, can not speak of particulars. Only enough has been learned to state that the seal of the Lord was here given to the work, in that souls were saved and the work of the Lord gloriously advanced. Zion's stakes were strengthened and the place of her tent enlarged.

The next work in which Brother and Sister Willis engaged was with the Methodist Episcopal Church at Norris Square, Philadelphia, with Rev. Thomas Harrison, pastor. Introduced to the people of this society in a providential way, as will be seen in another chapter, these evangelists at once found a rare opportunity to serve the cause of their great Master.

The brethren of this charge had just come to the close of their protracted meeting and were completely tired out, and a spirit of non-expectancy as to good results in the meeting prevailed. In the morning service of a Sabbath, late in November, 1884, Brother Willis was present and was asked to pray. In the evening, Pastor Harrison being unwell, he was asked to preach and to conduct the revival service. The Church had no adequate apprehension of the power that this man, supported by his noble wife, had with God. They knew not that one so skilled in the revival work and so irresistible in spiritual warfare was leading the movement that night. In his prayer, before his evening sermon, Brother Willis said: "Lord we ask thee for fifty souls. Father give, for Christ's sake, give us fifty souls." Having obtained the assurance in his own mind that his prayer was answered he declared his faith that fifty persons would seek the Lord that night. To some this seemed like mere empty talk, very extravagant language from a man most wonderfully excited. No one could feel that there could be five persons forward for prayers. In fact many were ready to laugh at his apparently nervous and excited words. But the evangelist never doubted, but laid hold on the promises of God that souls might be saved. The result justified the prophecy. God honored his great faith with mighty displays of divine power. Conviction seized the congregation, and on invitation for seekers of religion to come forward for prayer, the altar was crowded with anxious penitents, and when the count was made fifty-three had come for pardon and salvation.

The Lord thus providentially opening up the way and honoring in a most remarkable manner the faith of his servants. Brother and Sister Willis were now invited to remain and continue the work. From that time on the victory was signal and the Lord rewarded the faith of the evangelists, and crowned their labors with abundant success. They obtained great favor with the people of Norris Square, and for five or six weeks the meeting went on, until more than two hundred were converted to God. Owing to the fact that Pastor Harrison will speak of this work and of these workers in another place, we will not go into the details of this important revival service. But suffice it to say that from the best information that can be obtained, the people of this charge greatly appreciate the wonderful work that God wrought at the hand of these, his servants, and forever will hold them in greatful remembrance.

Their appreciation of them has already been shown in deeds of kindness and much material aid, both at the time of the meeting, and at subsequent times. It was here that God raised up friends true and tried, who did much to aid and cheer them on in their noble work. The evangelists ever afterwards held this Church and people in highest esteem. With this meeting at Norris Square M. E. Church, the evangelistic work of Brother and Sister Willis closed in America, at least, for the present.

The seal of the Lord was upon their special labors as evangelists until the last service of the last meeting in which they ever engaged together. With Brother Willis this was the last meeting of the kind that he ever held.

Although many churches in Philadelphia, and at other places over the land, were now open, and invited the services of these successful evangelists, yet they now heard the call of the great Master in another direction and turned their course to a foreign field.

CHAPTER XV.

How to Succeed in Soul-Saving.—Some Fail.—Mr. Willis always Won.—His Special Preparation.—Consecration and Acceptance.—Endued with Power.—Assurance of Success.—Peculiar Personal Endowment.—Methods of Work.—Faith of the Church.—Earnest, Intense and Continued Prayer.—Fasting. —Work for All.—Power of Song.—Use of Tracts.—Mention of Good done.—Fearless Preaching.—Expect Immediate Results.—Open the Way for Seekers.—Rejoice with the Converts.

In the pages which have preceded we have endeavored to give some account of the history and work of Mr. Willis, and have called attention prominently to the various revivals in which he has engaged with such uniform and unfailing success; how that in no place did he undertake the management of revival services without seeing souls converted and a revival ensue. From all the many fields in which he labored he always came with many sheaves.

Having closed the account of his evangelistic work, it may be well now to make some mention of the means and methods by which this evangelist, aided by his faithful and efficient companion, acheived such marvelous and certain success in a work so great, so important, and at the same time so difficult. A work before which so many ministers and pastors have quailed and found themselves powerless to accomplish. No problem has engaged the thought of the true minister more than how to save men; how to arouse the religious thought of communities and successfully to persuade men to be reconciled to God. It shall not be our purpose in these pages to discuss evangelism or to philosophize on methods of successful soul-winning in general, or to set forth extended observations as to the best methods of inaugurating and carrying forward great revival movements. But because the life-work of the subject of this narrative was largely in the field of revival work, we shall simply attempt to inform our readers of the methods pursued by this evangelist of whose life and labors we have undertaken to speak. In doing this we shall have a task sufficient, and should we succeed, a result that will be more valuable than any abstract discussion, from our pen, could possibly be. Fact is better than philosophy, and experience, than reason.

Concerning the work and success of Mr. Willis it may be said that while his methods were somewhat peculiar to himself, and his manner sometimes a little eccentric, yet the underlying principles upon which he moved, and the general principles of his action, were by no means peculiar, but were broad enough to fit any worker in any time. He brought to the work certain qualifications to which, in the beginning of this volume, we have already alluded, and on which it may be profitable here to speak still further. Before calling attention directly to his plans and methods of gospel work, we would notice some elements of his preparation. Among these we mention:

1. He was thoroughly consecrated and had the full assurance that he was accepted and accredited as an agent under God, to go forth as a soul-saver in a broad sense, and as an evangelist in a special sense. Before entering the field of work the question was fully settled that he was the Lord's and from henceforth to be led and directed by his divine hand. He had made an unconditional surrender, renouncing

self and every other master, to come into harmony with God and into full sympathy with his great work. His faith apprehended the fact that he had been fully accepted and authorized to act in the name of his Lord, in persuading men to be reconciled to God, and by all honorable ways, in season and out of season, to hasten the coming of Christ's kingdom.

2. He was endued with power and especially anointed. He felt that he was not only the Lord's by regeneration and adoption, but by special anointing for a particular work. When the fields opened and the call came for him to engage as an evangelist, he knew that it would be useless for him to go out without special equipment. He must have power from on high—a special baptism of the Holy Ghost for the Lord's work. This he sought and found—the pentacostal gift descended upon him in power. He realized in much assurance the special anointing for the work of soul-saving. A passion for souls then possessed and consumed him as never before. He obtained a conscious hold upon God and felt the Divine spirit was upon him to perfect his own Christian life—to enable him to be holy—to overcome sin, and to lead many others into the way of everlasting life. He was filled with the Spirit and thereby

consciously realized that he was empowered to meet the requirements of successful soul-winning and to do the work of an evangelist.

3. He possessed an assurance of success in the Lord's work, and went forth to his various fields of labor in the consciousness that if he was faithful in the use of the power which God had given him, success would be guaranteed in every step of the work. His faith overcame the world and he believed that the great Head of the Church who had commissioned him, would attend his work with victory. He relied on God through prayer, constantly expecting that the divine power would so accompany the word that it would not return void, but would accomplish that whereunto it was sent. Where his own strength failed he ever believed that the strength of the Lord was sufficient and always available to overcome the world, and on the divine arm he relied as confidently as a child upon a father. Herein he rested his hope of success. God had a work for him to do and he was clearly commissioned to do it in the name of Christ. He never doubted, that as it was needed, power would be duly and adequately furnished. To him God in Christ was ever present, and with almightiness standing by him there was a present realization of future

accomplishments. Like the apostle, he could say: "This is the confidence that we have in Him that if we ask anything according to his will he heareth us; and if we know that he hear us, whatsoever we ask we know that we have the petitions that we desired of Him." In this confidence Brother Willis never dishonored the Lord, nor retarded the divine work by doubts and unbelief.

4. One more element in his special preparation we mention, and that was his peculiar personality. He had natural fitness and adaption for the work of his calling, and great power to influence and persuade men. It was his nature to lead, and in a wonderful manner others would easily submit to his power and control. All his powers and gifts peculiarly fitted him for his work as an evangelist. He was young and vigorous in mind and body, of medium size, lithe of limb, attractive in countenance, possessing a clear, strong voice and a penetrating eye. All these powers helped him in the Lord's work. His gift of song was especially useful, for he mostly did his own singing and many were attracted by the music in his services. His eyes, powerful and earnest, were always an element of his strength. On one occasion, as he was passing down the aisle,

a very large man on whom he had fastened his eyes, began sinking down in his seat, saying: "Don't try any of your magnetizing powers on me." His peculiar gifts and strong personality eminently contributed to his great success in the work of soul-saving, and in his qualifications his natural abilities must not be over-looked.

Thus called and equipped for a special work, Mr. Willis began his work of soul-saving as a traveling evangelist in connection with and under the sanction of the Church of which he was a member, always engaging with local churches on invitation from the pastor and people. His work was entirely in harmony with the church; he never went out to work independently, and seldom went outside of the denomination of which he was a member. He was truly an evangelist of the Methodist Episcopal Church, and sought always to build up strong churches, by strengthening the things that were weak. Toward this end he ever labored, and left in his path societies harmonized, strengthened and enlarged, multitudes added to the church such as shall be saved. And here the question arises: How was such work accomplished? What were some of the methods by which Mr. Willis operated in his work among the various churches where he labored? The answer to this is somewhat difficult. His work can be better understood by seeing it, but a few things may be said that will aid the reader to a partial answer, at least, to this question and to a knowledge of the principal methods in the great work of bringing men to Christ. Prominent among the means used and methods pursued by Mr. Willis we notice:

1. That he sought to inspire faith and expectancy on the part of the church. Every invitation from a society or church was made a subject of most earnest prayer, and accepted only as it was clearly revealed that the Lord had directed and called. It was a settled principle with him to accept work only as the Lord directed, and when an invitation to labor as an evangelist with any society was accepted, it was because he believed he was acting under the call of God. With this faith, engagements were made, and at once it was an aim with Mr Willis to raise the faith and expectancy of the Church to the same point of his own. This he did sometimes before arriving on the field of labor, by letters to the pastor, declaring his own assurance that a good work was at hand and that he felt confident that many souls would be saved. To promote this faith, direction was often given to the pastor to begin meeting in

full confidence that a glorious harvest would be gathered. Accordingly faith was inspired, and under this inspiration the church would believe, and sometimes the work of salvation would be commenced before the evangelist had arrived. On coming to the field, quite often the revival was already a certainty in the minds of the church. The prophetic words of the evangelist were heard as a voice from heaven. He would proclaim that scores or hundreds would soon be saved. Not unfrequently whole assemblies, in answer to the question, would declare their belief that a great awakening was at hand. Preparations were accordingly made to carry on the work. The people would come together and multitudes would assemble as by magic. At other times less preparatory work was done and the work was inaugurated solely by the presence and personal efforts of the evangelist. However, seldom more than three days would elapse, and never more than a week, before the multitudes would gather and the revival would set in. The somewhat eccentric manner of the evangelist, and his intense earnest and startling declarations at once would surprise and arouse the religious thought of a slumbering community.

2. With the faith of the church at a good point and rising, he next sought to engage the church members and all Christians in most earnest, intense, and continued prayer for the immediate salvation of souls. Prayer was all important, and should the church cease to pray most earnestly, the work could not go on but must soon pause. The evangelist himself believed that the power of God stands ever ready to respond in answer to prayer, but it must sometimes be most importunate, intense, wrestling. Having once taken hold on God for a revival at a place his prayer continued until it prevailed, and as a result others would be incited to join in earnest prayer for the general and particular work of revival. To facilitate this object and to get the whole church and community to pray, Mr. Willis urged the duty of prayer at every meeting day and night, and appointed certain hours at which to fall on their knees, at least three times a day, to pray for the conversion and rescue of the unsaved and perishing. Sometimes a whole day was set apart for fasting and prayer. Fathers and mothers were exhorted to pray for their children, and children for parents, and "That prayer be made for all men, lifting up holy hands without wrath and doubting." To call more attention to this

part of the work, he sometimes asked that the bell be rung for fifteen minutes at midday, and while it was ringing the people should continue in prayer. At one place this was done with electrical effect. Conviction seized upon the people as never before and some were constrained to surrender to God in their homes or in places of business while the people were thus engaged at prayer on behalf of their unsaved friends. In all the work of Mr. Willis, much stress was put upon the fact that the people were praying, and he often attributed the lag in a meeting to the fact that the people were not continuing to pray. He believed, in a true and spiritual sense, that souls could be liberated from the bondage of sin in answer to prayer, by the same power that liberated Peter from prison while the disciples prayed. He believed that the same power was ready to save souls to-day in answer to prayer as accompanied the preaching of John Knox in Scotland, where his people had prayed all night for the success of the next day. Truly much prayer day and night by himself and the church was one of the essential means of victory in the work of salvation.

3. Work on the part of the church. Brother Willis also believed that God wanted to save the world through the work and service of

consecrated men and women. All were stirred to activity. By all means, professing Christians were urged to do personal work to advance the salvation of souls. They were induced to do this sometimes by personal entreaty, sometimes by special meeting for workers, sometimes by a startling command in the public congregation, and sometimes by suddenly dismissing a meeting on account of the inactivity or lack of enthusiasm on the part of professed Christians, who ought to be ready, in season and out of season, to witness or work for Christ, but who, too often, were not ready even to testify to Christ. The result would soon be apparent. The church members would realize their coldness and distance from Christ, and would come back to the next meeting alive and ready for duty, with courage, prayerfulness, and increased zeal.

4. In all Mr. Willis' meetings the power of song was made to do an important office, and used to powerful effect. This part of the service he generally led himself, with Mrs. Willis presiding at the organ, urging that the whole congregation take active part, which, under the lead of the evangelist, it was not difficult to persuade them to do. The whole congregation would soon sing as the people did in the days

of early Methodism. The gospel in song became a powerful agency in reaching the heart, and not unfrequently, under the inspiring songs of his meeting, souls would be converted while standing or sitting in the congregation. Mr. Willis depended much on the inspiration and enthusiasm of this part of the service.

5. The use of brief tracts, and small cards with significant words or questions on both sides became an important feature in Mr. Willis work. One card especially was widely scattered by the evangelist, and also put in the hands of the workers for distribution. It contained on the one side the great question,

"Are you saved?
If not, why?

On the other, Eternity!
Where will I spend it?"

Many were saved through this medium. In one meeting a man testified that he had been very wicked, but one day at his place of business somebody handed him one of these cards; he was going to destroy it because its contents so impressed him, but something held him back. He was startled, impressed and convicted, and went to hear the man who was sending out these cards and making such a stir in the city. At the meeting he yielded to God and was converted and said that the little card was the means of his salvation. Another into whose hands this card had fallen was converted by it and came to the meeting where he said: "I have often seen the advertisement, 'Rough on rats,' but that little card (holding it up,) is 'Rough on sinners.'" Mr. Willis did not use many lengthy tracts, but a card of the kind mentioned, brief and startling, he considered an efficient aid in awakening thought.

6. Another point in Mr. Willis' tactics was to make prominent mention of the good work already accomplished and at the same time keep up the expectation of great things to come. He always thought it proper to tell what God was doing for the people and to make mention of any encouraging event in the meeting, or elsewhere in the Lord's work. In other words "To noise it abroad" to the glory of God. If there was a daily paper that would report the work each day and tell of the souls saved he counted that an advantage. To sing the doxology when a conversion took place was not an uncommon occurrence. To tell of the good meetings just preceding the one in progress was deemed an inspiration to the present service. A prophecy of success in each meeting often

became the occasion of great faith and hope. On one occasion at the first night Mr. Willis encouraged the audience to expect fifty conversions. Their faith arose from discouragement, doubts gave way, and on the same evening fifty-three decided for Christ and bowed at the altar of prayer. Good cheer, buoyancy, and hope were prominent characteristics of his leadership, and were continually maintained. Everything available was turned to account to make successful the one work in hand—that of saving souls.

On this line of procedure, holding meetings with the various pastors and churches who had invited him, Mr. Willis succeeded. In all his meetings he proclaimed the truth boldly and did not shun to declare the "Whole counsel of God," at any cost, but cried aloud and spared not, expecting that there would be remarkable and immediate displays of divine power, accompanying the word. It is not too much to say that he seldom, if ever failed to see an immediate result, such as justified the highest expectation. Communities were thrown into an anxiety for salvation at once, and sinners in great numbers were brought to decide for God.

His aim centralized in bringing men to decision and salvation. It was expected that at every meeting some would decide to seek Christ. Accordingly at every meeting the way was open for seekers to present themselves at the altar of the church, or to arise for prayers, or go into an inquiry room, and not unfrequently interested persons would linger after church services and bow in prayer with the evangelist or other workers just where they happened to be. With Mr. Willis, any time and all places were suitable to commit souls to the service of God. Good impressions were not allowed to wear away. Whenever penitents were found, there must be no delay in inviting and pressing them to immediate decision, and the opportunity for them to do so must never be wanting. When conversions took place they were duly recognized, and seldom would one be saved without the personal knowledge of the evangelist, who, at the time, or soon after, would greet the convert with much satisfaction and joyous delight; often the fact would be announced to the assembly and all would join in singing the doxology over newly converted souls.

In the execution of these plans, it will be remembered that Mr. Willis was aided by his devoted wife, who, in consecration and faith, was never lacking but was always a source of strength and support to her husband in the great work in which he was engaged. She always fully co-operated with him, to render all his methods and plans efficient and successful. Her manner was different from his, but in the means and methods employed in the revival work they were a unit, and fully enjoyed each others confidence and support.

CHAPTER XVI.

The Missionary Impulse.—Correspondence with Bishop Taylor.—The great Sacrifice required.—The self-surrender to work in Africa.—The Pledge demanded.—The engagement for work in Africa.—The Brooklyn Convention.—His Usefulness there.—An Inspiration to the Convention of Missionaries.—Account of Manager Rev. D. G. Griffin.

It was while laboring in the evangelistic work in Philadelphia, that Brother and Sister Willis decided to extend their usefulness to a foreign field. They were both given to the Lord, and whatever would be the divine will, they were ready to undertake. They had often talked about the Missionary work and had often felt a deepening desire to carry the gospel to the benighted and heathen lands. Very early in the life of Mrs. Willis the missionary impulse possessed her, and arrangements once or twice, as has already been noticed, were completed for her to go as a missionary. But while being hindered and delayed, the desire never left her.

Scarcely less was the desire of Mr. Willis upon the same subject. He had long contemplated foreign work, and felt called to do missionary service.

They had both had an early acquaintance with Bishop Taylor, who once before had taken the name of Mrs. Willis for his work, and who was now launching the great enterprise of raising a missionary band, which he expected to lead into the centre of Africa, and establish a line of missionary stations in the Dark Continent, commencing at St. Paul de Loanda and extending through the interior. Mr. Willis now communicated his desire for a place of service in the missionary field, to Bishop William Taylor, who was already well acquainted with Brother and Sister Willis, and who replied in the following interesting letter:

NEW YORK, November 18, 1884.

DEAR BROTHER AND SISTER WILLIS:

Your favor of the 12th inst. received and considered. The only place open to you in my work just now is the Dark Continent. I have no knowledge of what shall befall us there. We propose to enter at St. Paul de Loanda, 9° south of the equator. Our objective point will be the Tushelange country, about one thousand miles from Loanda. Now whether the Lord will leave us travel a thousand miles to place of beginning or have us begin at place of entrance and establish a line of stations from the coast to the heart of the continent we know not.

Our conditions for Africa candidates are, 1. Passage paid to the field of labor. 2. When settled down in a new field to depend on God and his African resources for subsistence. 3. To draw their salary at heaven's exchequer when the day's work is done and heaven becomes our home. The privations and perils are too great for any one who is not so conscientiously called of God as to invest his life in it. We don't go to die but to live and labor for God; but to die cheerfully if the Lord shall deliver us *to* death, that he may deliver us *from* death.

We shall dwell in tents as did Isaac, Abraham and Jacob. No conveyances on our line of travel except to carry ourselves on our own legs. All our things have to be carried by men. I am having small trunks made covered with tin. The trunks to weigh about sixteen pounds. Contents of our clothing, books, etc, forty pounds —fifty-six pounds a man's load. Our people can send their things in any rude box to care of Baker, Pratt & Co., 17 Bond Street, New York, and then pack in the small trunks.

Each passenger can have one or two of these trunks. They can ship larger cases to Loanda and take the chance of leaving or losing them there.

Now dear Brother and Sister Willis if you can face the dark side of the fact and possibilities of this work, and feel sure that God calls to Africa, then you may consider yourselves engaged. I have to go in ten days, my party not for two or three months.

Your Brother,
WILLIAM TAYLOR.

This opportunity with all its perils Brother and Sister Willis duly considered and were ready to comply with its awful requirements and undertake the work. They felt that it was the open door that God wanted them to enter, and accordingly they were willing to go and put their lives, if needs be, into this great Missionary enterprise. They loved Christ and his church above their own lives, and were willing to undertake great and perilous things for his name's sake. The engagement was at once made and they became subject to the call of the Bishop, who expected that his company of missionaries would start from New York for Africa on the 22d of January, 1885.

However, before the departure of the missionaries, a holiness convention for missionaries to Central Africa was called to be held in Carroll Park Methodist Episcopal Church, on Carroll Street, Brooklyn, New York, Rev. H. C. McBride, Pastor, to begin Thursday, January 15th, at 10 o'clock A. M., and continue one week, when the expedition was to sail for Loanda, via. Liverpool, by the Inman Line, from Pier 36, North River, New York, at 9 o'clock A. M.

At the call of the Bishop, Mr. Willis and wife arrived at Brooklyn from their field of labor at Philadelphia, and reported to this convention at the beginning, ready to enjoy its blessing and to further its interests in any way possible. It was soon ascertained that their services might be turned to good account in the work of the convention.

In this convention both Brother and Sister Willis took some important part and received overflowing blessings. During these meetings Mrs. Willis records in her journal, some things with regard to her work and experience. Once she says: "We had a most precious meeting to-day. Truly this is tarrying in the upper room." In another place, January 18th, she says: "Our last Sunday in America. Rev. A.

Lowry preached this morning a most profitable sermon from James, 5:20, 'Let him know that he which converteth a sinner from the error of his way, etc.' I am so glad that I am one of the soul-winners. Dear Father help me to improve every opportunity."

On Sunday afternoon of the convention, Mrs. Willis spoke, and much power attended the word; many, and especially mothers, sought heart purity, and with tears in their eyes, rejoiced in the help the words of the speaker had afforded them. On Monday evening, January 19th, she was requested to conduct the altar services, when God again blessed the word, and the altar and five rows of seats were filled with seekers, some for pardon and some for purity.

On Sunday evening, January 19th, at Sand Street M. E. Church, Mr. Willis preached his last sermon in America. The society had asked the convention for a preacher, and Mr. Willis was sent. A glorious meeting was had, souls sought God, and the pastor wished that Brother Willis might remain to conduct further revival work.

Rev. D. G. Griffith, the conductor of these meetings found in Mr. Willis a brother dearly beloved and a helper that he greatly prized.

On being requested to write a few words concerning Brother Willis for this volume, the following valuable tribute was cheerfully furnished:

"The subject of this volume came to the Brooklyn Convention convened by Rev. A. E. Withey and Bishop Taylor, direct from the field of victory, Philadelphia, bringing his devoted wife and only child, anxious for his field and work to which he felt that God had called him. Africa was on his heart, he was devoted to God, to his family, to sinners and to his work as an evangelist, especially, now, to Bishop Taylor's expedition; he believed in the Bishop. He was full of love, full of faith, he believed readily, he spoke easily, lithe in body he moved easily, quickly. He saw no obstacles to one's being instantly saved and wholly. He himself being wholly consecrated and received by Christ was as he believed wholly sanctified. The week alloted to the departing missionaries from New York was a busy one, and yet he seemed best pleased when in the real work of soul-saving. Speaking from the pulpit, praying up the aisles, calling men to have faith now at the same time joyously praising God that 'it comes,' is coming 'still' and again speaking to have faith now, now. He was an inspiration in the convention which we could hardly have dispensed with, and can never forget. He was quickened by the Spirit to discernment, he seemed never to find his place so much as the glorious life he had within found in him a heavenly place. Young, medium height and weight, face pure and white, hair dark, eyes full and earnest, and loving to look into, salvation was his cry, Africa at any and every cost. His universal thought and desire were to go into the Dark Continent to show them God. He would not think of small means, nor stop at half measure. His was a whole burnt offering."

CHAPTER XVII.

Departure for Africa.—The Voyage.—Entertainments on Shipboard —Storm in crossing Atlantic.—Arrival at Liverpool.— Kindness of Fowler Brothers.—On board Steamship Biafra. —A Coast Storm.—Mrs. Willis' protracted illness.—Kindness of Friends.—Maderia Island.—Sierre Leone.—Conversion of Mr. Wilson.—A Wedding at Sea.—Crew boys.— Meeting Bishop Taylor.—Landing at Mayumba.

The convention having closed, the missionaries were to present themselves with all necessary outfit and equipments at Pier 36, North River, New York, on January 22d, at nine o'clock A. M., to sail for Loanda via. Liverpool, by the Inman Line steamship. Accordingly Brother and Sister Willis with their little boy, not two years old, were at hand and ready to sail with the out-going company.

The feelings and hopes of this devoted band of missionaries, as they left their native shore may be seen more clearly from a few words which we here quote from a page in Mrs. Willis' journal, written on board the Steamship Montreal, which carried them to Liverpool enroute for Africa. In it under date of January 22, 1885, she says: " Set sail this morning from Pier 36, on steamship Montreal for Africa. Our party are all happy and well. Last night at our farewell meeting we had a most precious time. Truly this has been a tarrying at Jerusalem. Rev. William M'Donald of Boston was there and gave our party words of cheer. Bless God, we rejoice to go to Africa. This morning while the dear ones were standing on the dock, weeping and waving a fond farewell we felt more like shouting than weeping, many did shout, Mr. Willis among the number. We feel that it is a great privilege to be a member of Bishop Taylor's first expedition to central Africa; our war cry is 'Africa for Jesus.' May the Lord God of Joshua go before us as he did before him, and give us the hosts of central Africa for himself, and the same God give us the same promise. " Have not I commanded thee? Be strong and of good courage; be not afraid, neither be thou dismayed, for the Lord thy God is with thee whithersoever thou goest.' My promise for to-day is beautiful—The eternal God is thy refuge and underneath are the everlasting arms."

The voyage across the Atlantic Ocean, from New York to Liverpool lasted eleven days, and for the most part was a stormy one, and sometimes perilous. Mr. Willis from on board the vessel after a severe storm, January 28, 1885, writes: "We are all safe in the arms of the Almighty. Yesterday we had indications of a storm. I was anxious for it—anxious to see the power of the ocean. Some shrank back a little but I was anxious for it to come. I knew that our ship was a good strong one and that we were in the hands of God. The sea became very high in the afternoon and continued to increase until night. We thought at night that the ocean was nearly at his best but in this we were mistaken. I only partially undressed when I lay down for the night—Spent all the afternoon and a greater part of the night in watching the waters. Toward night the waters frequently swept over the deck. Some of us got a taste of salt water and in return came near giving salt water a taste of us. As night came on the storm increased to a fearful hurricane, and our vessel seemed to strain every timber to withstand the force of the sea. Wife and I talked until about half past one o'clock at night, when I fell into a little doze. At two o'clock I was awakened by the most frightful noise you could imagine. It seemed as if the ship was being ground to pieces between mighty ice-bergs, and every timber groaned. She quivered—she struggled—a crash—a roar—and in much less time than I can tell it the waters came surging through below. Every passage, every state room—pantry, cabin, and everything was flooded. I was not slow in getting into my clothes and protector. I then rushed from my room. I had not a thought of fear, yet, I was waiting to hear the cry: 'To the life-boats.' Kissed wife and Ossion, telling them to stay in their berth until I saw the extent of the damage. I was almost first in the halls, several others appearing about the same time. We were in a sad plight. No one knew then where the break was or its extent. I soon discovered that the companion way had been crushed in by an aft wave, but did not know what else had been damaged. We were soon in line and bailing out water, and oh, what a time. For an hour and a quarter we strained every nerve to get the water bailed out. We dipped about twenty-five pails per minute. After that we worked with more ease for another hour or two when we were relieved to praise God and rest while the sailors finished. They could not come to our relief for nearly an hour. Many things were spoiled on board. Our boatswain was washed overboard, and thrown back on deck by another wave. Two of his ribs were broken. Through all this storm and danger, Jesus kept us from fear and we are all right." This vessel had crossed the Atlantic one hundred and eight times, and the captain said that he had never witnessed such a storm before.

After this storm was over the rest of the voyage to Liverpool was quite pleasant. The weather became more settled, the sky was sometimes cloudless and the sea quite calm for the time of year.

The experiences on ship board were not confined to sea sickness and storms, for there were many delightful entertainments. The early morning prayer service was conducted by Rev. A. E. Withey of Massachusetts, to whose fatherly care was committed the entire missionary party. After breakfast was served all who were able, took a stroll on deck, then came the morning assembly for bible study. As the officers of the steamer daily consulted the chart that they might avoid the ice-bergs, the rocks and the shoals, and bring the vessel safely into port, so these faithful servants of God out on life's ocean, sought the chart of His blessed word, that their voyage might end in the haven of eternal rest. Rev. Charles Radcliff of England, was among the passengers, and having devoted much study to the proper training of children and the simplified methods of primary instruction, he conducted each morning a "phonetic method" class for the benefit of the children on board, of whom there were twelve or fifteen. In the afternoon there was a short discourse by some one of the missionaries and in the evening a short sermon was delivered, to which the steerage passengers were invited. Mr. Willis preached several times in the evening during the voyage across the Atlantic. "My word shall not return unto me void" had here a precious fulfilment, for many of the steerage passengers professed conversion. Mrs. Willis was so ill she was not able to attend many of these services.

The voyage across the Atlantic was completed, the vessel reached Liverpool on the night of February 1st, and the company landed in safety on the morning of February 2d. Mr.

Willis writes from Liverpool and says: "We are here at last. Find this a wonderful, stirring city, full of life. Our voyage across the Atlantic lasted eleven days. Most of the time we had storms, but bless the dear Lord we are all here although we suffered much and were in great peril. If God had not been with us we should have perished."

On their arrival at Liverpool they were met by members of the firm of Fowler Brothers, wholesale produce merchants of that city. They carry on an immense business, and have several branch establishments, one of which is located at Cincinnati. These gentlemen are deeply interested in Bishop Taylor's work in Africa and are the representatives of his work for England. They are widely known for their Christian benevolence and philanthropy. The entire party were conveyed at once to the Hurst Hotel where the Fowler Brothers had generously arranged for their comfort and entertainment.

On Wednesday, February 4th, after a stay of but two days in Liverpool, Mr. Willis, wife and child embarked with the missionary company on board the steamship Biafra, bound for Loanda, on the West coast of Central Africa. The course of the vessel was to be by the way of Gibraltar, Maderia Islands, Liberia, stopping at the most important towns along the West coast of Africa until it reached Loanda.

After the departure of the vessel from Liverpool a storm was soon again encountered and the company for some days suffered extremely so that almost every one on board was sea-sick. The storm was so severe that for two days and two nights the fires were washed out almost as soon as they were kindled, and on one night the ship masters did not try to run the vessel, but only kept the bearings. The seamen said that they never had encountered such a severe and continued storm.

At Liverpool many friends urged Mrs. Willis to return to America as she was so greatly reduced through sea sickness. She felt however, that having suffered so much from this cause in crossing the Atlantic, she would not be troubled from it in the future. The first day out she was again stricken down however, and throughout the days of the storm her sufferings were terrible. On one occasion the officers of the Biafra carried her from the stateroom into which no fresh air had come for three days, and while the rain was falling in torrents, they strapped her to a chair and lashed it fast to one of the masts of the steamer. Wrapped in a great rubber coat with the winds whistling above her and the waves washing over the decks, she thought of Him who " Maketh the storm a calm" and prayed for the hour when He should say " Peace, be still." When she returned to the stateroom Mr. Willis was occupying the upper berth also very sick. In fact nearly all of the seventy passengers were sick during the storm, including the doctors.

The coast steamers can accommodate comfortably, about twenty-five passengers, but from the large number of missionaries and traders on board every stateroom was crowded. Mrs. Willis in this very trying hour while wishing in her heart for some greater comforts, thought now and then of the loved ones in the land of her birth and the home of her youth, surrounded by all that can make one peaceful and happy, but there was no shrinking from the duties of the hour or a single regret for the step taken for the Master. If a cloud passed over her sky it was immediately dispelled by the sweet consolations of Paul, " My God shall supply all your needs." Phil: 4-19.

Captain Thomas very kindly sent his steward to Mrs. Willis, after her return to the stateroom, expressing his sorrow at her extreme illness and insisting that she should vacate her room and accept the use of the Captain's cabin during the rest of the voyage. A kindness so marked could not pass unnoted.

As the vessel approached Madeira Island, Mr. Willis writes: "This is a most beautiful day, a clear sky and so warm that we are as happy as bees in midsummer. Everybody is on deck to-day. Some time to-night we will get to Madeira and land in the morning, so that we can visit on the Island for four or five hours. Then we shall get plenty of banannas, oranges and grapes. We shall make stops all the way down the coast."

While all were assembled on deck singing their praises to Him who " plants his foot-steps in the sea and rides upon the storm," and chatting together over the deliverance from the ocean's yawning mouth, Mrs. Willis was for the first time introuduced to the traders on board, of whom there were several, on their way to their trading stations along the coast.

The vessel touched at Madeira after a stormy voyage of eight days and stopped until the next day at 3 P. M. Mr. Willis and wife, together with others, improved the opportunity of landing and enjoying very much the scenes of the Island and rest in the city of St. Ann's. Here they felt as though they would like to live and die. It was a land of beautiful scenery and of high mountains, with fruits and flowers, almost the year round. It was truly a Summer land—attractive in the extreme.

After their return to the steamer much amusement was caused by the divers who had come out in their canoes in great numbers to exhibit their skill in diving for six pences and other coin which was thrown for them into the water. The kindness and respect for Mr. and Mrs. Willis by the traders was manifested in many ways. Magnificient boquets of flowers and baskets of the choicest fruits were bought on board for them, and just before leaving, a boat pulled along side of the steamer and an elegant bamboo invalid chair was lifted to the deck, and while all were admiring it, one of the traders kindly said: "Mrs. Willis, are you pleased with it?" "Who do you think it is for?" Of course she could not tell, and without waiting for an answer, he said: "Your friends have purchased it for you. We are sorry that you have been so sick and still suffer so much and we will esteem it a favor to have you accept this slight token of our regard, and will thus permit us to add to your comfort."

From the anchorage at Madeira Islands, the ship sailed on its course at 3 P. M., February

12th, and the next day about noon passed the beautiful snow-capped mountain of Teneriffe, one of the Canarie group, two hundred and forty miles from Madeira. Its top is covered with snow while at its base is a real Summer.

It is not strange that Mrs. Willis sometimes wondered what God's purpose could be in permitting her to be sick so much while on the way to labor for Him. But "He moves in a mysterious way, His wonders to perform," and there came a day when she saw His righteous purposes unfolded and sweet was the flower of her ripened experience. Among the passengers was an English gentleman by the name of Wilson, (an assumed name.) By his noble, manly bearing and reserved manner, he won the respect of all. He was introduced to Mrs. Willis at the same time she met the traders on the steamer. He was somewhat shy of the missionaries as were the traders generally, but one afternoon he met her on the upper deck and engaged in conversation. After inquiring concerning her health and expressing his sorrow at her prolonged illness, he said: "You should have taken the advice of the Captain when you were about leaving Liverpool and have returned to America. You are entirely too delicate to withstand the ravages of the African climate.

What do you hope to accomplish among such degraded heathen? You ought to return as speedily as possible and let these poor Africans take care of themselves. I don't believe in this missionary business any how. I am a free thinker." She felt in a moment that God had sent this poor soul to her for spiritual guidance. How could she convince him of his error? Quick as the meteor's flash, the words of inspiration came, "Not by might nor by power, but by my spirit saith the Lord." She realized that no time must be lost in argument, so sending a prayer heavenward for direction, she related to him the following simple but touching story: "In a certain home, a sweet, bright eyed little girl of eight summers was the pride of the father's and mother's hearts. The mother was a devoted, faithful, Christian woman, but the father was an infidel. He tried to teach the child the principles of infidelity, but for the mother's sake permitted her to attend the Sabbath school near their home, saying, 'it cannot do her much harm."

One day the little daughter was taken sick and at her request the Sabbath school teacher was sent for and prayed with her. The doctor pronounced her disease black diptheria and gave but little hope of her recovery. Two days after, she was taken much worse and the teacher was sent for again. The mother sat by the bed side, fanning the fevered brow of the little sufferer, while the father was pacing the floor in anguish of mind. Suddenly the little one called her papa to her side and taking his hand she said in a voice so strangely sweet, 'Papa, you have often told me that there was no God, no Saviour, no heaven. Mamma has taught me that Jesus came all the way from heaven to save everybody who would love him. She has taught me that there is a God and a home in heaven for all who are good. The doctor says that I must die, that I cannot get well. I feel that I am dying now. Papa, as I am going away so soon, what shall I do? Shall I take your God or mamma's God?' The father with heart almost breaking and the scalding tears streaming down his face, said: 'Oh, my darling, take your mother's God! take your mother's God!'"

When Mrs. Willis had finished the story, Mr. Wilson was weeping bitterly, and without a word abruptly left her and actually ran down the deck. She sent heavenward a prayer that God would touch his heart as the story had stirred his emotions. Mrs. Withey having noticed Mr. Wilson weeping asked Mrs. Willis if she had been talking to him about his soul, and when she learned the cause of his strange action said, "It is wonderful for I see he is under deep conviction." Mr. Rudolph said, "Now my sister I begin to see why God has so afflicted you." Mr. Wilson soon returned and said, "Oh, Mr. Willis, what made you tell me that story! what made you tell me that story!!" If you had known the history of my life you could not have told it better. I am not a free thinker. If any one ever went to heaven my wife has gone there." He then told her the story of his life. He was the son of wealthy parents in England and had been an officer in the Royal Navy. Some years before he had married a sweet christian lady, but after seven years of happy wedded life she died. A few months after he buried his little boy only six years old, his only child. At the grave he cursed God because of his desolation and bitter sorrow. He became a wanderer and a profligate, and was breaking his father's heart. He spent a good part of his fortune. He deserted the Navy and went to India. Not thinking it safe he started for America, on his way he met an actress and they went to Australia. He was so miserable he had left his wife in Australia, and feeling that he had ruined his life and brought sorrow to those he loved, he was now going down the coast to die." Mr. and Mrs. Willis pointed him to Jesus Christ the sinner's friend and gave him a copy of the little book, "Daily Food" containing so many sweet promises of God which he promised to read. He landed at a station between Bonny and Old Calabar, and two weeks after he died of hasty consumption.

No other stop was made until the African coast was reached at Sierra Leone. Here their ship arrived early in the morning of February 19th. An opportunity was now offered for any one to land that desired, but as Sierra Leone was said to be a very unhealthy place on account of African fever it is commonly called the "white man's grave," nearly all the company refused to land. But as the ship was to lie anchored for six or eight hours, Mr. Willis thought it a splendid opportunity to go ashore. Mrs. Willis could not go, but stayed on board to keep the child Ossian. Accordingly, with some traders and fortune seekers, Mr. Willis landed on the African shore about nine or ten o'clock A. M. Accompanied by a young German gentleman from Indiana, U. S. A., who was on his way to the Congo, near the Equator, he called on the American Consul,

Mr. Lewis. The Consul and his excellent wife invited them to breakfast, and the hospitality was accepted. The breakfast, Mr. Willis pronounced good. It consisted of liver, poached eggs, bread and butter, tea and coffee, greens, onions, oranges banannas, and many other palatable things, such as the climate and soil produced. After breakfast they were entertained with piano music, singing, and instructive conversation. At the request of Mr. Willis, the consul and wife visited Mrs. Willis and child on board the vessel before the departure from Sierra Leone.

Mrs. Willis writes as follows. " Our next stop was at Moravia, at which place we expected to take Bishop Taylor on board, the Bishop having preceded the expedition one month to Liberia, to preside over the M. E. Conference at Moravia, on the Liberian coast. It was near evening when we anchored off Moravia; but soon after anchoring, one of the large surf boats was lowered, and a number of the gentlemen of our party accompanied by the Bishop's son went on shore to meet the Bishop. Meantime those on board found plenty to interest them, scores of little canoes were lying alongside, whose occupants were clambering up the ship's sides like monkeys, uttering exclamations of surprise at seeing so many 'white mammies and pickaninies,' keeping their eyes open for a chance to steal anything they could lay their hands on. But the cannon on the forecastle is booming, a signal for return and soon the splash of oars is heard, and we gather in joyful expectancy on the upper deck to welcome our beloved Bishop. Our joyousness is turned to keen disappointment when good Brother Withey informs us that he has gone on to Cape Palmas to visit our mission station there, and await our coming. We are now running along the "Kru" coast, and every few hours we drop anchor, from two to five miles from shore, the canon booms again and again, and through our glasses we can see natives hurrying to and fro on shore, canoes are launched through the surf, and in a remarkably short time are alongside. Then commences a big palaver between traders and Kru boys. Kru boys are natives living just below the coast of Liberia, and are employed by the traders as far south as Mossamedes to manage their surf boats. The steamers always anchor from two to five miles from the beach and it is necessary for the transfer of cargoes, etc. that experienced hands should man the surf boats. The Kru boys have been employed from the time of the first Portugese settlement on the West coast, and are chosen because of their being expert surf swimmers and for their great muscular power.

By this time we have become quite well acquainted with the traders on board, among them a Mr. Evans, returning from a visit to his family in Wales, to his trading station at Mayumba. Mr. Evans has become very much interested in our expedition, and is very anxious that Mr. Willis and myself should stop at Mayumba with him and establish a mission there.

On the 22d of February we reached Cape Palmas, a delegation from our party and several of the traders go on shore to meet the Bishop. Our anxiety to see him has become so intense that we can do nothing but stand on the upper deck and watch for the surf boat which is to bring our party to the steamer. Far in the distance she comes gliding over the waters, every eye is strained to see that one dear face. Ah! there he is, see, they are waving their hats, and now we hear singing. The boat comes alongside, we gather near the railing of the upper deck, the Bishop is coming up the steps, it is the same majestic form, the same kingly bearing, the same holy countenance— our Paul of the nineteenth century. Every eye is dimmed with tears of joy while "Father Taylor" embraces each one of his faithful band. Words of mutual love are spoken and then "Praise God from whom all blessings flow" bursts forth from every lip. It is Sunday morning, a perfect tropical day, and as we all gather on deck to listen to an excellent discourse by the Right Rev. Deacon Hamilton, Episcopal Arch Deacon of Africa, we feel that

> "Heaven comes down, our souls to greet.
> And glory crowns the Mercy Seat."

Our next stop is at Bonny, at which place Arch Deacon Hamilton leaves us. He had most favorably impressed every one on board, as a noble, christian gentleman. We pray God to spare this good man's life many years to continue the work he has accomplished in the region of the great Niger, where for twenty-five years he has faithfully toiled, establishing important mission stations and by his consistent life has won the universal esteem of the coast traders. It was at Bonny that I had my first real glimpse of life among the West African natives. One morning our kind Captain Thomas asked me if I would not like to take a little trip down the river, in the Biafra's steam launch and visit a native village. As I was much improved in health, I told him it would afford me great pleasure, so I don my bush suit made of light weight blue flannel and consisting of pants, cut by a Philadelphia tailor, kilt skirt falling to the knees, and blouse waist, high boots of alligator tops and kangaroo bottoms, tropical hat, made of light India cork, and am ready. No! wait a minute I have forgotten my big umbrella. There now, I am ready. Our steam launch and two small boats have been lowered, so have the steps from the upper deck; but all of the party are not going; so good-bye for a few hours. Now, then we are seated in one of the boats, several of the traders in the other, a stout rope is attached from each one of the small boats to the steam launch. Now, my good Kru boys, look out, watch your paddles, or there will be a collision, which must be avoided, as these waters abound in man eaters. And though we imagine an American missionary would be a dainty morsel, we have no desire to be served up in this style. While we have been talking about the sharks, our boats have left the steamer far in the distance. Let us take a look around us. Native canoes dot the water here and there. Yonder are several ships from far distant ports lying at anchor; on either side of the river, in some places the dense tropical vegetation crowds the low banks; in others, marshes and mangrave swamps abound, but our boats are headed for the shore, and as we wish to learn something about an African village, we will go with them. The Kru boys have lifted their paddles, but how are we going to land? Surely we are not going to wade ashore? While these queries have been running through my mind, several of the Kru boys have jumped into the water; one of them backs up against the end of the boat and Captain Thomas, who like Zacheus was short of statue, but instead of climbing into a tree, climbs on a Kru man's shoulders, and sitting astride is carried safely ashore, as I see my dignified friend doing this act so nicely, my sense of the ludicrous is awakened and I mentally ejaculate:

> 'O wad some power the giftie gie us,
> To see ourselves as ithers see us."

Captain Thomas has been giving one of the Kru boys some instruction and he steps up to the boat, takes me in his arms, and carries me to shore, as carefully and tenderly as if I had been a babe. We rest a few minutes and then start into the bush. Which way shall we go? Ah, here is a narrow zig zag path; let us see where it will lead us. We go about a half mile when we come to a sort of fence made by placing tall posts of bamboo close together, which have sprouted out forming quite a baracade; inside of this enclosure are two or three dirty, shallow cisterns, here the path is intersected by another, both leading into the dense bush, we take the one to the left and soon reach the village. An old woman spies us and disappears into a hut, pretty soon the fetish doctor comes out and comes toward us. Then begins a gesture palaver on both sides and soon we make him understand that we want to walk through the village. He first offers us some mimbo (palm wine) but we refuse it and walk on. O, what a foul, dirty place, a few odd looking porkers are lying around or walking in and out of the huts at pleasure, and two or three lean dogs snarl at us. Their huts, the largest of which can't be more than sixteen feet by twenty feet are built of clay, and thached with grass or bark. The villagers themselves, wear scarcely no clothing, the very small children none at all. They seem to be thriftless, dirty and lazy. As we leave the village some of the women run after us begging. I yield up every loose bit of apparel I have with me, and hastened away, as their clamoring makes me feel uneasy. We are again carried to the boats and return to the steamer.

The next morning we anchor alongside of an immense hulk lying in the river, and while our steamer is being lightened of some of her cargo, we accept a cordial invitation from the trader in charge of the hulk to hold a meeting on board, and enjoyed an excellent Bible reading conducted by the Bishop.

Under date of February 26th Mr. Willis writes: "We stopped at Monrovia Saturday night. Took Bishop Taylor on board at Cape Palmas on Sunday morning, the 22d inst. We have on board one hundred black men, some of them cannibals. Nearly all of them are naked, except that they wear a small piece of goods about their hips. Hundreds came out in canoes to see us. Their canoes are a sort of hollowed out tree. Many came on board and bought such articles as they needed. They call our ladies "white mammys." Our boat is now lying to at Bonny. A chief came aboard this morning, and also, a great many natives. This afternoon the king is coming, he has 150 slaves for oarsmen. At 3 P. M., Mrs. Willis and I are going ashore. A trader has given us a boat and as many oarsmen as we wish. We have everything we need. Mrs. Willis and I are very well. One of our company is very sick from typhoid fever. A number have had African fever. The climate seems to agree with us perfectly well and we are happy. Yesterday was a big day on board. We had a wedding, wife and I were bridesmaid and groomsman. The upper deck was enclosed with English, National and Individual flags, and as the parties were from the United States, the stars and stripes were over us. The ceremony was according to the English custom, and as soon as it was over about fifty men began throwing rice at us and oh, such a time. They had a tubful and they used it to the best possible advantage."

Under date of February 25, 1885, Mrs. Willis writes: "A wedding on the sea. This has been a day of excitement. At half past two this afternoon Rev. C. L. Davenport was united in marriage to Miss Mary Myers, M. D. a graduate of Boston Medical college. This morning the upper deck was decorated with all the ship's flags, etc. At half past one the heavy cannon on the forecastle began booming, and continued at intervals of every ten minutes until the bride and groom had taken their places before the officiating clergymen. Rev. Hamilton, Arch Deacon of Africa, Church of England, and Bishop Taylor of M. E. Church of America, performing the ceremony. Husband was the groom's best man and I was bridesmaid. Every one is having a gala day. Missionaries, traders, stewards, sailors and even the Kru boys are celebrating the event in some way or other."

We reached Old Calabar on Saturday evening. On Sabbath morning we go on shore and proceed to the Scotch Presbyterian Mission, in charge of Rev. Anderson, a saintly man who has spent his life in mission work—forty years of which had been given to the work at Old Calabar. They have excellent mission buildings. Most of the material having been sent from Liverpool for their construction. The currency of the natives consists of bent pieces of wire. They look very much like an immense hair pin, or croquette wicket, these the natives wear or string on one arm, before going to the native market. I walked about quite a little on Sunday, and towards evening began to feel very ill. On Monday, dear Father Anderson secured a hammock and two carriers and I was taken to the boat and conveyed to the steamer. I shall never forget how, when Father Anderson bade me good bye he placed his hand upon my head and with tears running down his cheeks, gave me his blessing. On Monday morning our captain took Bishop Taylor and some of the party up the river in the steam launch. After leaving Old Calabar I was ill for many days. And though our steamer touched at several places I did not again go on shore until we reached Mayumba.

Under date March 4th on board the steamship Biafra Mr. Willis writes: "The day is very beautiful, temperature about 110° in the sun. We are passing St. Thomas Island, bordering on the Equator. We spent Sunday and Monday, March 1st and 2d, at Old Calabar, on a river of the same, about forty miles from its mouth, and not far from the mouth of the Niger. Mrs. Willis, is very sick. I think the sun was too strong for her. To-day she seems better but is very ill. Ossian is well and strong and happy as one could wish. I am well but very weary.

Just after day-break this morning we passed Princes Island and Three Brothers. The latter are very small, and seem to be only high rocks rising out of the water. We are now very close to the Equator and will soon cross; we are just now coming to the shore of St. Thomas and will remain a few hours. Wife is still very sick." On March 6th the vessel anchored at Gaboon, on the African coast, on the Equator, and on the 9th reached Mayumba, 2° 3' South Latitude and 10° East Longitude, on

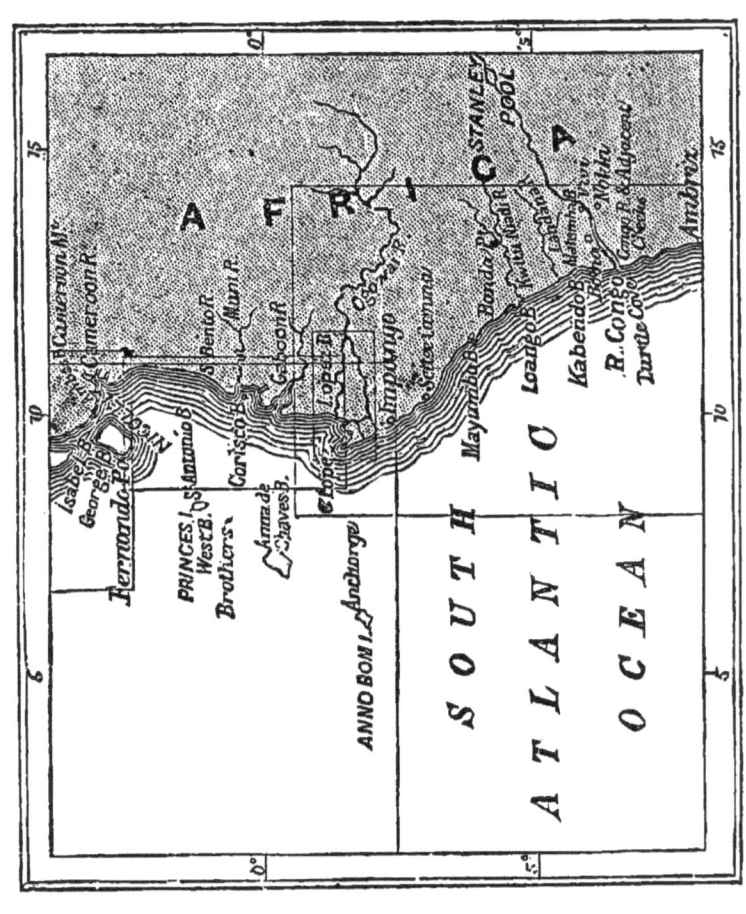

the west coast of Africa and two hundred and fifty miles north of the Congo River."

According to a new arrangement on board the vessel, Mayumba was to be the starting point for a future missionary station. It was no part of the original plan that any missionaries should be stationed here nor any place north of the Tuscolange country but the entire company under Bishop Taylor were to land at St. Paul De Loanda, and thence proceed into the interior, forming a line of stations. But owing to what was deemed a providential opening, the Bishop concluded to set off missionaries and establish a mission at Mayumba. This new arrangement was effected on this wise: On board the steamship Biafra, were a number of coast traders, returning to Africa from Liverpool; among them a Mr. Evans, a man of means and influence, called along the coast of Africa "The white king." This man importuned the Bishop to establish a mission at his place, Mayumba, making the offer to board and sustain the missionaries one year without charge. The offer after much prayer and deliberation was accepted and regarded as a providential call for the establishment of a mission in that quarter. To this station Mr. Willis was appointed as minister in charge, with his wife Mrs. Anna Willis as assistant. The following certificate bears testimony of their office and appointment:

"This is to certify that I, William Taylor, a Bishop of the Methodist Episcopal Church, have this ninth day of March, 1885, appointed Henry M. Willis, preacher in charge of a new mission now to be founded on the self-supporting plan at Mayumba, W. C. of Africa. I have also appointed his wife, Mrs. Anna C. Willis, assistant Missionary, both being accredited ministers of the gospel, as evangelists in the United States of America. They go purely on the gospel plan of self support—" The laborer is worthy of his hire"—to be paid by the people who get the benefit of their labors.

I commend these dear young persons and their little boy to the confidence and consideration of the people with whom they may associate."

"William Taylor,
March 9, 1885.   Mayumba, W. C. of Africa.

At the same time, Mr. F. B. Northam one of the Bishop's company from Connecticut, and a Mr. Stickleman a German from Indiana, lately converted were set off as associates, to found a plantation some place up the Mayumba river for a mission farm school. Mr. and Mrs. Willis were the first of our missionaries to be vested with authority and credentials of ministerial office and Mayumba was the first mission station established by Bishop Taylor on the west coast of Africa.

Mrs. Willis says: "Our steamer cast anchor in Mayumba bay before daybreak and Mr. Evans said as I made my appearance on deck in the early morning, "Welcome to Mayumba." I looked toward the shore, it looked very picturesque as I stood there. On a narrow strip of glistening white beach were four or five traders' houses. Back of these flowed a beautiful river dotted with several small islands.

From the opposite bank the land seemed to slope gently into high hills, covered from the base with dense tropical forests which I learned afterward were almost impenetrable to white men The preparations for landing had all been completed and the Bishop together with part of the missionaries were to accompany us on shore. The boats were furnished by the captain and Mr. Evans, and at the signal from the cannon on the forecastle the Kru boys put out from shore and were soon by the side of the steamer. In a large basket chair suspended from the yard-arm we were lowered into the boats.

Joyous expectation was mingled with the sadness of parting from friends who were bound to us by many sacred ties. The tearful "good-bye" on commencement days of classmates whose months of school life have woven the friendships tie forever; the strange "farewell" of the soldiers whose weary months of toil and conflict have forged the tie of brotherhood seemed united in our experiences. Together we had sat at the feet of the Mighty Teacher. We had studied side by side the lesson of christian duty. We were soldiers of the King Immanuel and in his service of toil of conflict and of victory we were made one in purpose, one in life, and one in Christ.

The fervent "God be with you till we meet again," and Old Hundred's Praise God from whom all blessings flow," rent the air. The hands were uplifted, the heads were bowed and the benediction pronounced. A scene so strange and memorably sweet it comes as an inspiration as I write. The captain and officers of the steamer and the traders went on shore with us. Carriers came to the surf and I was lifted into a hammock and carried to the house only about three rods distant. It would have been impossible for me to walk through the white, hot and glistening sand. I found soon that the sand was quite deep and very trying to the eyes. We landed about eight o'clock in the morning, and after lunch, the company made an inspection of our station, and about three o'clock they were escorted to the boats and amid the waving of handkerchiefs, and singing, and cheers, we bade them God speed.

CHAPTER XVIII.

The Steamer leaves Mayumba.—Temporary Home with Mr. Evans.—Sunday Morning Services in Mr. Evans dining-room.—Visit to Mamby.—Mr. Willis and Ossian attacked with African fever.—A visit to the Native Villages.—A visit from King Mamby and many Natives.—Customs of the Natives.

As soon as the steamer disappeared from view, Mr. Willis and I go to our room and kneel in fervent prayer, that God may bless our coming to Mayumba.

The house of Mr. Evans, which is to be our home for the time being, is a low, square building, roofed with bamboo, and built on a foundation of oyster shells with a veranda all around. It is cool and spacious, and stands on a sandy beach with the sea about twenty-five rods in front, and the Mayumba river about six rods in the rear. Just across the river, or lagoon, is a beautiful wooded country, which abounds with wild cat, deer, monkeys, gorillas, and other animals which inhabit this region.

Mr. Evans proves himself an excellent host, and we are all made to feel at home. During the afternoon Mr. Evans calls the boys together that do the housework, hands a large bunch of keys to me, and instructs the boys that while I remain there I will have full charge. In the evening, the white residents of Mayumba, and Mamby, of whom there are some ten persons outside of our missionary party, met at Mr. Evans, and we passed an hour or two very pleasantly in getting acquainted. The Bishop had sent a small Mason and Hamlin organ ashore, and after music and singing, Mr. Evans invites us to have prayers, to which all remained, and having expressed their good wishes for our health and success bade us good night. We retire to rest, and notwithstanding the hardness of the bed, troublesome roaches and other discomforts that cannot be remedied, we sleep very well. At half past six the bell rings for "tea" at eleven we will breakfast, at four have "tea" again and at six dinner will be served. As our house boasts of but little furniture, I have decided to try and make things look a little more homelike, which, with the aid of some bright calico, a few boards and the valuable assistance of willing hands, is accomplished in a few days.

Our culinary department is sadly in need of reformation. Mr. Evans employs a native cook, who reigns supreme in our gally (kitchen) a little low building, about one rod from the back door, built of bamboo sides, and thatched roof. Here he displays his skill in doing problems in curry, palm oil, red peppers, garlic and goat's flesh, which I am anxious to investigate. So one day I announced my intentions to Mr. Evans, who solemnly informs me that I will never eat another meal prepared by "cook" if I do. But on again expressing a desire to make things as homelike as possible he went with me to the galley to give cook orders to do whatever I said, warning him that he would receive a severe flogging if there was the least complaint, which, of course I was careful to avoid. That morning I did my first cooking in Africa; but I had a sorry time. The substitute for a stove was merely a shelf built of bricks and clay some 3 ft. high, 8 long and 3 to 4 wide, on one end of this shelf was built a clay oven, which was minus a door. As cook could not understand a half a dozen English words, I called Ponsua, Mr. Evans head house boy, to interpret for me. I then told Ponsua in pigeon English. to tell cook to make me "plenty much fire one time." Meantime investigation had revealed to me several iron pots and frying pans, in different stages of cleanliness, which I proceeded to have washed. I then told Ponsua to have "plenty much fire made in them oven, and when them fire get plenty big take them out one time," which direction elicited loud exclamations of surprise from cook, who had been in the habit of making a big fire in the oven and putting right in the fire and smoke what he wished to roast, sending it to the table smoked and burned on the outside and raw on the inside. After he had removed the smoking brands I had him scatter the red hot coals over the bottom of the oven, procure a piece of canvas for a door, and by breakfast time was able to have a nicely cooked roast served. But meantime the smoke from the fire on the shelf had been causing me great discomfort causing the tears to stream from my eyes, so that when I emerged from the galley I was nearly a smoked missionary. The breakfast was pronounced by our traders to be a grand success. And indeed they ate as if they enjoyed the meal hugely. Our meals were always served in courses, roast goat, stewed goat, fried goat, rice, etc. Between each course the boys took the plates out on the veranda and

FACTORY AND NATIVE EMPLOYEES.

brought them back clean. (?) On one occasion after my plate had been returned, I happened to notice the marks of a tongue as it had faithfully done its duty round after round in "licking the platter clean." I looked up at Mr. Evans who was laughing at my evident consternation, and said, " Begging your pardon, I ask the privilege of not having my plate changed between the courses, as I prefer to have my plate licked but once.

On Saturday, the Kru men scrub the floors. We have no scrub brushes or brooms, so they use a piece of fibrous wood about the size of a brick. First the room is cleared of everything but the bedstead, upon which are piled garments and all sorts of articles, then a lot of white sand is scattered on the floor, which is then deluged with water, and then eight or ten Kru men get down on their hands and knees, side by side, each one seeming determined to scrub but one plank, working to the time of the song they are singing. It is characteristic for the Kru boys to always sing while at their work. If they sing fast they work fast. If they sing slowly they work accordingly.

On Sunday morning, Mr. Willis holds services in Mr. Evans dining room for the traders, and in the evening preaches to the natives and

Kru boys. On Monday, Mr. Evans took Messrs Northam and Stickleman, to Mamby, (distance seventeen miles up the river from Mayumba) to select land for a mission plantation, but returned inside of three days each suffering from an attack of African fever. The next morning Mr. Willis and Ossian were both suffering from the same cause. I struggled bravely against the symptoms, but before six o'clock I was compelled to take to my bed. In a few hours I was delirious, Mr. Willis too ill to lift his head, and poor little Ossian lying in a stupor. Good, tender-hearted, Brother Northam, had by this time passed through the heaviest of the attack, and though very weak, crawled out of bed, and installed himself as nurse. Mr. Willis was the first to recover, then Ossian and in a few days I was able to walk about the house, but we were much reduced in strength. This was our first real experience of African fever (with the exception of the slight attack I had suffered on the journey down the coast) but it was not our last, for during the remainder of our stay in this deadly climate, we were subjected to repeated attacks of the fever. Still I firmly believe that with proper medical attention and plenty of wholesome food, such as we are accustomed to in our native land, that the white man can live on the West Coast of equatorial Africa, if he is willing to sacrifice the comforts of civilization. I am sure much of our suffering was due to the lack of proper medical care. Mr. Evans had a medicine chest; but neither the traders or our party knew much about prescribing; so we continued to take our daily portions of quinine as the Bishop had advised us. One night Ossian awoke us by his moaning, in a few minutes he was rolling over the bed in agony, which was followed by a deathlike stupor, a cold perspiration breaking out on the entire surface of the body, we thought he was dying, and with sinking hearts continued to apply restoratives until through the blessing of God, the crisis was past; at another time he remained for ten days in a stupor, taking but little nourishment, but these trials, or the discomforts we had to endure did not make us wish to leave the field of labor to which we had felt called.

We had now been residents of Mayumba several weeks, and notwithstanding our illness had started a school on a small scale, at Mr. Evans house, but finding our facilities for work in this direction very much cramped, we decided to take a trip to Mamby, visit some of the native villages, and assist, Brother Northam, who had by this time begun the building of a small mission house, to establish a school. So one night we take advantage of the tide, and about ten o'clock we are assisted into one of Mr. Evans large boats, in which are already seated around the edge a number of Kru boys. With a shout the boat is pushed off, the Kru men begin a wierd song, and ply their paddles to the time of the music (?). If they sing fast, they paddle fast, if they sing slow, they paddle slow. The night was an intensely dark one, I could not distinguish the features of Mr. Willis' face, though he was sitting by my side. I could not repress a slight feeling of timidity when I remembered that on this same river, only a few months before, three officers from a " man of war" ship which had stopped at Mayumba had been drowned while hunting hippopotamus. They had succeeded in wounding a hippopotamus, which had so enraged it that it craunched the end of the boat with its teeth and trampled the bodies of the unfortunate officers in the mud and reeds. While I was thinking of these things, our boat came to a sudden standstill, and what with the excited shouting of the Kru men and the darkness, there was considerable excitement until a lantern was lighted and we found we were only entangled in the long reeds. The Kru men succeeded in getting back into the channel without upsetting the boat and inside of another hour our men began to shout " Miveza" which we found out was the name of Mr. Whites native linkster at Mamby. A linkster is a native employed by traders, who intrust them with a small quantity of cloth, rum, etc., with which to go into the " bush" and barter for rubber, ivory, palm nuts, etc., with natives living back from the coast; but the linkster is generally shrewd enough to leave the cloth in his own village, and start out with a few pounds of salt which coast nat.ves make from ocean water, and which is considered a great luxury by the natives further in the interior.

While we have digressed for these explanations, Miveza, (which means smoke,) has been awakened, answers the call and soon a light appears at the top of a hill, which seems to rise abruptly from the water's edge, we land, and begin the ascent of the slippery, winding path, and when about half-way up meet a couple of carriers with a hammock, to carry me the rest of the way, but thinking that I would be safer on my feet, than in a hammock at such an incline I insisted on walking to the top. A hammock is merely a piece of canvas about eight feet long and three to four feet wide, with a curved piece of wood, something the shape of a half moon fastened on each end, then fastened by a few ropes on to a bamboo pole some ten to fourteen feet long and carried by two men.

The next morning we arise early, eager to see the place by daylight. As I gaze from the front door, I am charmed with the scenery. The house which is constructed mostly of bamboo surmounted by a thatched roof is situated in a little clearing on the top of the hill we ascended last night. At the foot of this hill, hemmed in on either side by the dense green foliage, runs the river, its ripples, dancing and sparkling in the sunlight. As my gaze passes rapidly from object to object, it at last rests on the ocean, which is about one mile and a half distant, the roar of the surf sounding musical at this distance. Delighted with this view, I cross the room to the back door; in a clearing surrounded by tall forest trees and dense bush, is built a "galley" and three or four bamboo huts. "The "galley" is the trader's kitchen and the huts belong to his native employees. There are two trading houses at Mamby, the one owned by Mr. Evans, in charge of his clerk, Mr. White, and one belonging to the firm of Adson & Cookson, England, in charge of Mr. Carns. During the morning Mr. Northam received a note from Mr. Carns asking us to breakfast with him which invitation we accept, and a ten minutes ride in our " mission canoe" presented to Mr. Northam by Mr. Evans brings us to the bamboo home of Mr. Carns built in a little clearing on the river bank. The first thing that attracts my attention on nearing the landing is a banana grove. A number of natives rush out into the water to help pull the boat nearer the landing, while some native women stand in the background, eagerly watching Ossian and I. During the morning we are visited by quite a number of natives.

After enjoying a good breakfast and pleasant visit at Mr. Carns, we return and in the evening Brother Northam, Mr. Willis and myself have a precious scripture service and prayer meeting. The next morning we are visited by a great many natives from surrounding villages, among them King Mamby and his wives some twenty in number. When I went out to see them they set up a cry, and several ran away, but soon gathered around me and I shook hands with them all, they seemingly enjoying the performance very much. Most of them were smoking short clay pipes, though I noticed that some of the women who were not had their pipes stuck in their hair. King Mamby's head wife, the oldest and consequently in Africa the ugliest of his wives, took a dirty pipe out of her mouth and after putting some fresh tobacco leaf in, took a whiff and courteously handed it to me. Of course I refused, meantime illustrating by gestures how it would affect me, at which they set up a perfect howl of laughter. She then asked me through Miveza the interpreter "if white man smoke in my country?" I told her yes. "Does white mammy smoke in your country?" No, white mammy no smoke? " Well, if white man smoke why white mammy no smoke?" which argument I did not try to answer.

In the afternoon my sufferings became so intense I had to go to bed. For from the time of my first attack of African fever until I left Africa I was so ill, that at times I was almost helpless, and entirely incapacitated for work. Mr. Northam and Mr. Willis had been waiting patiently for me to get strong enough to visit some of the native villages, so one night I told them I would be ready to go the next morning if I did not feel any worse; the next morning bright and early the hammock was gotten ready, Mr.

White providing the carriers, and we start.
The native employees on finding that " white
mammy" is going to visit King Mamby, all go
along, also a number of villagers, and some of
Mr. Carns " boys." We take the main road
to Mamby's town, the main road being a mere
foot path, so narrow that travelers are obliged
to go single file. The first part of the way,
leads through a dense strip of tropical forest,
which however soon emerges out into a winding
valley covered with a heavy growth of tall, dry
grass, higher than the tallest of the carriers,
but here my observations for the time end, as
the carriers are running full speed, meanwhile
all hands keeping up a constant bedlum of
noise, with their shouting and singing. I try
to hold up an umbrella, but finding this out of
the question, pull my cap over my eyes, to keep
out the blinding rays of the tropical sun. I then
try to make them understand that I would like
to go slower, but they think I am only gestur-
ing my enjoyment and run the faster. All
this time one of the number runs by the side of
the hammock, displaying his skill in bounding,
leaping, dancing and fantastic gestures.

Suddenly the carriers came to a stand still,
and sitting up I saw I was in the midst of the
village; and right glad I was to get out of the

hammock, for the carriers had run from the time I got in until they stopped in front of King Mamby's hut. While waiting for Mr. Willis and Mr. Northam to come I had quite a long "palaver" with King Mamby, Miveza acting as interperter. After they had reached the village, I had opportunity to look around me. Their houses ("shimbacks") which were built of bamboo, were very small, the largest not exceeding sixteen feet by twenty feet and six to eight feet high. The only means of ingress or egress was through a small aperture, or door in the front, which was so low that one had to stoop down to see inside. In one I found two women squatted on the floor making a grass mat. In another a woman was preparing cassada. With the exception of a few calabashes and clay pots the shimbacks were mostly devoid of furniture.

But time was precious and I had hardly begun my observations before the gentlemen were ready to start, and we left the village accompanied by the villagers dancing, singing and haloaing; but as we came in sight of the next village, they returned. This was repeated at every village at which we stopped.

While resting in one of the villages, our attention was attracted to a man in the distance leisurely walking toward the town, his hair seemed to be arranged in a peculiar manner looking as if three horns grew out of his head, but on his coming nearer, we discovered the supposed head dress to be nothing less than an inverted clay cooking pot blackened by long use. He carried a gun on his shoulder, on the butt end of which stood a squeaking parrot, the man was the village hunter just returning from the " bush" where he had gone in quest of game. The natives here are very fond of animal flesh, and if obliged to eat nothing but vegetable food for several weeks, have a positive craving for meat.

This craving after animal food, at times, becomes almost a disease. It attacks white and black men alike. Mr. Evans says that those who suffer from this strange craving become almost wild beasts at the sight of meat, which they devour with intense eagerness. I suppose this is the reason why every village has at least one hunter, and right proud he is to be the possessor of a trade gun. Owing to their contact with white traders, they present a strange mixture of savageness and civilization. Take for instance, their mode of managing fire arms. A trade gun is really a wonderful though inferior article of the old flint lock kind. As it is made to suit native ideas, it is rather large and heavy.

When a native cocks his musket, he wrenches back the hammer with a tremendous jerk; when he wants to carry home the game that he has killed, he suspends it from the muzzle of the gun; he then slings it over his shoulder and as he walks along allows it to bang against the trees. I have several times seen Mr. Evans hunter return from the " bush" with one or two monkeys, hanging to the muzzle of his rifle. He very well knew that we did not indulge in monkey stakes, but as he did, he generally took good care to use Mr. Evans powder to replenish his own larder. Some traveler truthfully says, " That it is in loading the weapon that the native most distinguishes himself." First he pours down the barrel a quantity of powder at random, then rams upon it a tuft of dry grass, upon the grass he puts some bullets or bits of iron, then some more grass, then more powder, grass and iron as before. It is not surprising that a gun should burst after such a method of loading, but it is strange that it can be fired at all without flying to pieces. Though the recoil may almost dislocate the shoulder, he likes plenty of noise and is satisfied.

But I have been digressing. Leaving this village we returned to Mamby, so well-pleased with our short journey that we resolved to visit other villages. So on the morrow we started again. When we reached King Mamby's village he was holding a palaver with the chiefs of surrounding villages.

As soon as my carriers stopped they all surrounded the hammock, and King Mamby lifted me out in his dirty, greasy arms. While coming through the tall grass, numberless little white stickers much resembling "Spanish needles" were frequently showered upon us and their sharp ends were causing me much discomfort. Noticing this King Mamby and his chiefs began leisurely picking them off, reminding me of an old woman picking a goose. After picking and brushing to their hearts content they turned the hammock inside out and gave it a thorough brushing also. While they were talking and gesticulating around me so closely I could hardly breathe, I felt myself suddenly jerked out of the circle. King Mamby's head wife had gathered the women together to give me a welcome, and she did not intend that her duskey admirers should monopolize all of my attention.

She led me to a group of women, reached out her hand and shook hands with me herself and then bringing the women up one by one, she kept my arm going something after the style of an old-fashioned pump handle, until I had shaken hands with every one of them. After having examined myself and my apparel to their hearts content, I was permitted to join the gentlemen who were conversing with King Mamby and the chiefs. Leaving them to finish their palaver we visited several other villages in one of which the chief insisted on our drinking mimbo (palm wine) with him. It was not fresh, and hence was as nasty and sour as yeast. In fact, the mission ladies at Old Calabar substitute fermented palm wine for yeast in making bread. The natives are very fond of palm wine, and indeed it is very pleasant and refreshing when new, but the reverse, to a European palate after it has stood a few hours. I have seen mimbo obtained in the following manner. After the tree had been cut down, a cavity some six or eight inches long and nearly as wide was hewn out with a matchet (native knife). Of course the sap would ooze into this cavity, which they generally kept covered with palm leaves. Here it remains until it ferments.

After remaining a few days longer at Mamby we returned to Mayumba, feeling that we now knew enough about our people to work among them to better advantage than ever before, and feeling eager, as were also the villagers, to open a school at Mamby.

The color of the natives in this part of Africa is usually black, but individuals among them are a dark, warm bronze, rather than black, many of them possessing quite regular features. They wear grass cloth if they can not procure cotton cloth, but whenever they can get a piece of print or "taft" they will wear it as long as it will hang together.

The grass cloth here is made from the cuticle of young palm leaves, stripped off skillfully by the fingers. It is then woven on a rude loom. Rev. J. G. Wood gives the following good description of a West African loom: "A bar of wood, about two feet in length, is suspended horizontally from the roof of the weaving hut and over this bar are passed the threads which constitute the warp, the other ends being fastened to a corresponding bar below, which is fixed lightly down by a couple of forked sticks thrust into the ground. The alternate threads of the warp are divided by two slight rods, the ends of which are held in the fingers of the left hand, which cross them alternately, while the wool is interlaced by means of a sword shaped shuttle, which also serves to strike it down and lay it regularly. In consequence of this form of loom it is only possible to weave pieces of cloth of a limited length." Enough of these pieces are sewed together to make a strip of cloth about three yards long and one yard wide. The manner of wearing a strip of of cloth seems to be left much to the fancy of the wearer. Braclets of brass, iron, wire and ivory are worn around the arms. I counted nineteen iron rings between the wrist and elbow on one woman's arm. Rings are also worn about the ankles. One woman had two heavy brass rings on each ankle, and seemed to be particularly pleased with the clanking noise she made while walking. The men are fond of covering their heads with a neat cap made of grass; they also carry a little grass bag, which they sling over one shoulder. It answers the purpose of a pocket, and is therefore very useful where so little clothing is worn. Mr. Willis purchased one of a native, which is made of some kind of cord, no doubt received in barter

Both sexes have about the same style in arranging the hair, some wearing it cut quite close to the head while others bead it into numerous little plaits, which, on account of the wooliness of the hair and the amount of oil and dirt, stick out all over the head like so many skewers. But the Kru boys are more artistic in the arrangement of the hair. First an elaborate pattern is marked out on the head, the lines of the design are then closely shaven, leaving little patches of wool scattered over the head, reminding one of the laying out of Central Park (small animals not excluded.) The principal food of the natives is the cassava, which is prepared so that it passes into the acid state of fermentation. Cassava greatly resembles a yam or sweet potato in appearance. After the root is dug it is placed in water for several days until it becomes sour, when it is ready for use. The women have one way of preparing it which is rather disgusting to a European. They make it into little balls looking very much like a cod-fish cake, by rolling it on their dirty, greasy chests. I tasted some that had not gone through the natural pie board process, and when Brother Northam asked me how I liked it, I told him I thought it tasted something like limburgher cheese smelled. They also have plantims, bananas, quavas and pine apples in their season, while fish abound in the rivers. They are so fond of animal food that they will eat it when almost falling to pieces with decomposition. But, in spite of their love for it, almost every kind of meat is prohibited to one family or another, or at all events to some single individual. One man dare not eat monkey's flesh, while another is prohibited to eat goat, and a third is forbidden to touch pork. On one occasion I offered Ponsua some pork, but he refused to eat it. I was so surprised that I insisted on knowing the reason, and he told me it was "Fetish." He believed that if he ate it, he would be bewitched and die. The terror which is felt at the least suspicion of witchcraft often leads to cruel deeds. Almost every one that dies, either by violence or a natural death, is thought to have been bewitched, and a "witch palaver" is held to find out the sorcerer. Sometimes the accused is compelled to drink a decoction prepared from the poison bean.

For example, a child of a slave woman belonging to a Portuguese trader died. The mother accused another slave woman of bewitching the child, a witch palaver was held, and the accused woman was compelled to drink poison bean from the effects of which she died in great agony. Another way of punishing "witch palaver" victims is to cut off the head with a huge native knife called a matchet. One day among a number of natives who had come to see me, Mr. Evans pointed to one of them saying, "That man is the head witch doctor of this country, and a more cruel beast never lived, everytime he has a victim sacrificed he drinks some of the warm blood." And truly, I had never beheld a more repulsive, brutal looking visage in my life; his face was hideously marked with red clay, and he looked such a veritable demon, that I shuddered. With the natives here, superstition takes the place of personal religion, and in spite of its dreadful consequences, it does, nevertheless, keep before them the idea of a spiritual world and impresses upon them the fact that there exist beings higher and greater than themselves. "Jimby," Mr. Evans interpreter, gave us much information concerning the beliefs of his tribe. According to his accounts, the country is overrun with spirits, but the evil far out-number the good, and the natives pay their chief reverence to the former, because they can do the most harm. They hang all manner of strange fetishes about their persons, some of which are supposed to protect them from some special danger, others to give them good luck; even the children are absolutely laden with fetish ornaments. They are made of all sorts of things, such as scraps of rags, leopard's claws, peculiar beads, bits of bone, horn, ivory etc. By the way, I have heard the word "fetish" explained as a " corruption of the Portugese word Feitico, *i. e.* witchcraft or conjuring."

King Mamby is as superstitious as any of his followers. He never stirs without his favorite fetish, which is made of a few civit cat skins, medicine bags and native iron bells; this he wears hung over one shoulder. He considers the jingling of the bells a powerful charm against evil spirits. Mr. Willis, after much palavering, prevailed on him to part with this fetish; when first asked to sell it he seemed horrified at the idea and gesticulating wildly demanded " Why no ask for King Mamby?" After showing him a number of articles, such as would gladden the heart of a savage he concluded to part with his body guard charm for a small clock, which he thought a most powerful fetish. As far as I can learn the mode of government which prevails through this part of Africa is something on the patriarchal order. A tribe is divided into a number of sub-tribes, each of which reside in a separate village, which is called after the name of its chief; the most powerful chief of the tribe receiving the name of king. King Mamby, himself, is scarcely distinguishable from his so-called subjects, his houses and mode of living being about the same. All the weapons I have seen are the spear, bow and arrow, matchet and club. I have several spears in my collection. Their shafts are about six feet in length and of very light weight; their heads are of various shapes, one of them is quite plain and leaf shaped, while others have a single pair of barbs under the head; still another has several of these barbs set just under the head. The bow and arrows, in my possession are very small. The arrows are merely little strips of wood some eight inches or so in length, and about the fifth of an inch in diameter. About one inch of each of the sharply pointed ends have been dipped in poison. The least puncture of the skin with one of these poisoned arrows is said to cause fatal blood poisoning. A matchet is a native knife, the sharp-pointed blade is about fourteen or sixteen inches in length and two inches wide with a handle some five or six inches in length and four inches in diameter. These are kept very sharp, and when not in use are kept in a sheath, made of bamboo or the skin of some animal. Every native, man or woman wears one of these matchets at the side. With the matchet, the women cut fuel for their fires and bamboo for their houses, dig plantaum, cut up the cassada, etc. The people here are not warlike but kindly disposed to those who treat them well, and we have learned to dearly love them. They are very eager for information. Every time Mr. Willis leaves the house he is surrounded by a group of natives begging him to teach them "about them God" and to "savva them white man's mouth." We find them to be very apt scholars. As the way is hedged up for us to have a school here Mr. Willis has promised "the boys" that we will go to Mamby in one moon's time, for they make all their reckoning of time to consist of so many moons but do not seem to be able to count beyond twelve moons, hence they do not know their age; neither have they any idea of the division of the day into hours.

CHAPTER XIX.

Bishop Taylor urged to request Mr. and Mrs. Willis to return to America.—The request made and accepted.—The arrival of the North bound coast steamer "Biafra."—The kind offer of Captain Thomas of the "Biafra"—Mr Willis' farewell "palaver."—Anchored at Old Calabar.—Mr. Willis again attacked with African Fever.—The course of the vessel ordered far out to sea.—Brother Willis fast losing his hold on life.—His last words.—His death and burial at sea.—Mrs. Willis almost crushed with sorrow.—Kindness of Captain Thomas and his officers and men.—Arrival at Liverpool.—Took passage on steamship "Servia" for New York.—Arrival at Philadelphia.—Memorial Service to Brother Willis.

As the gathering clouds betoken the coming storm, so the frequently repeated attacks of African fever told alas, too plainly what the end must be. Though Mrs. Willis had fought so bravely against the disease, her one great enemy, yet she realized that her life was fast ebbing away. The kind friends at Mayumba knowing that argument with her would be useless, wrote to Bishop Taylor, then at St. Paul de Loando, urging him to request Mr. Willis to return to America with his suffering wife, for it seemed more than a pity that she should remain there and die when it might be possible that God would permit her to do much for Him in a genial climate and christian land. The arrival of the Bishop's answer gave to Mr.

and Mrs. Willis the idea that perhaps God's voice was calling to a new and very important department of the African work. Some one should return to America and represent the work to the people at home. After earnest consultation and fervent prayer it was decided that if an opportunity was afforded Mrs. Willis and Ossian should come home and as strength returned she was to urge upon Christian people the great importance of the work in Africa and secure aid in the erecting of buildings for the present needs of mission work and perhaps be instrumental in directing the minds of other missionaries toward that vast field already "ripened for the harvest." With that resignation which only comes through consecration they prayed and planned and waited for their Lord to make plain the path of duty. On the morning of the 7th of August, the Kru boys brought the tidings of the expected North bound coast steamer being sighted. Soon the booming of the cannon from the steamer "Biafra" gave the signal that the freight must be ready for shipment without delay, and within an hour the anchor was dropped at Mayumba.

When Captain Thomas learned of the serious illness of Mrs. Willis he said, that although he had not the authority to give a free passage on the steamer, yet if Mr. and Mrs. Willis would accept his offer he would with great pleasure take them to Liverpool, and if the steamship company desired them to pay they might have two years in which to discharge the obligation. If they remained, Mrs. Willis must certainly die and it was doubtful about her reaching Liverpool alive. Under all circumstances Mr. Willis must accompany her both for the sake of his wife and child as well as for his own good and the Master's cause. The great kindness of Captain Thomas was accepted and he had the ladies cabin speedily prepared for the reception of those whom he had only a few months before learned to love as God's children. But two or three hours were given for the transfer of the freight and by the time the last boat load was being taken to the steamer, brother Willis had completed his hasty preparations and had called around him some of the natives for a " farewell palaver." Words can not express how deeply these poor natives were affected at the thought of parting with their " Preach man and white mammy." They realized that true friends were leaving them, those in whom they could trust, to whom they could turn for help, and who had taught them that there was a power beyond a " Fetisch," even a God of mercy and love. With tears rolling down his dusky face, one of them said: "Massa Willis, when you be go for dem Wee Country, who palaver black man about dem God? Who show black man him no lie, him no steal, him be plenty much good? Black man sabe dem trader man, him be devil man. Massa Willis him be plenty good, him love black man, him palaver black man about dem God."

When the boat was leaving the beach many tears of regretfulness were shed and brother Willis spoke the sentiments of his heart when turning to his wife said "Kitty, I feel worse at leaving these dear people who are hungering for God's truth, than of leaving our own dear people at home when we started for Africa."

Tenderly they were lifted to the ship's deck and comfortably stowed away in snug quarters. What a flood of memories thronged them. Only a short time before they had left that steamer for a life work, but a strange change had come over their sky so bright with promise for the future. They could not murmur but would ever hope and trust for the Friend above all others whispered so sweetly, "Lo, I am with you always."

The vessel was to stop as usual at important points along the coast and after seven days at sea they anchored at Old Calabar not far from the mouth of the Niger. During the three days stay at this place Mr. and Mrs. Willis shared the hospitality of a Mr. White, one of the leading merchants of Old Calabar. His beautiful home betokened an ease and refinement far beyond anything that they had met since leaving Liverpool. The kind attention combined with the many home comforts made their visit delightfully pleasant. They visited the missionaries at this port and met among them Rev. Mr. Anderson, whose christian labors there had extended over a period of forty years.

Before the time of departure had come Mr. Willis gave signs of returning fever, and much sickness was reported on board the steamer. As pleasant as most of their visit had been on shore, on returning to the vessel Mr. Willis was stricken down with African bilious fever. In consequence of so much sickness the captain ordered the course of the vessel far out to sea hoping that there would be relief as soon as they should get away from the unhealthy port, and beyond the deadly miasma of the Niger. But for brother Willis there was no permanent relief. After four days of suffering from alternate chills and fever, the disease began to assume its worst form and on the 21st of August, he became alarmingly ill. The kind attention of the sailors and all on board knew no bounds. The captain watched as closely every change in the sufferer as he did the movements of the steamer. His sympathy towards every passenger who was in any distress was always manifested, but Mr. Willis had awakened in his heart the deepest of human sympathies for he loved him as a brother. He anxiously paced the deck and his sharp eyes quickly searched the surgeon's face as he would come each hour from the bedside of the sick one. Every known remedy was administered, and every one was ready in a moment to aid the ship's doctor and carry out his slightest wish.

It soon became evident to brother Willis that he was fast loosing his hold on life, and nearly all about him felt that his final hour was near at hand. The hush of all merriment when the sailors were off "watch." The subdued tones in which the ship's orders were given; the strange silence for a "steamship under way," told more plainly than words the solemnity of an hour which may be felt but cannot be spoken. During these days Mrs. Willis was at times so ill she could not leave her berth, but the fresh invigorating sea air was strengthening and the recurring attacks of the fever were less frequent. The critical condition of Mr. Willis greatly alarmed her and she was buoyed up by her anxiety for him. She fanned his fevered brow, calmed him in his hours of wild delirium, sang and read for him in his conscious moments, and talked to him ever of their blessed Lord and Master, Saviour and Friend, JESUS. The tender sympathy of friends was sweet to him but the singing of his dear wife was far more sweet, and in his extreme weakness he would try to sing with her.

Who but those whose hearts have bled can know the struggles of that patient sick and weary watcher as she sang for him whom she loved, realizing too that in a few short hours he would leave her forever and would himself join in the songs of the Redeemed in glory! With voice tremblingly sweet, lips faltering, heart throbbing, sobs choking, and scalding tears streaming down her face, she sang, "Nearer my God to thee."

More precious than the singing was the WORD to him. He would repeat passage after passage of scripture, now a precious promise and again some word of blessed assurance and comfort. The African work rested very heavily on his heart and he prayed earnestly that God would send others to take up the work which to him was so full of promise.

He frequently expressed the desire that if God was pleased to spare him, he might come to America and secure at least ten missionaries to go back to Africa with him and establish a chain of missions across the continent from Mayumba to the Baptist mission stations on the Congo. During one of his lucid intervals while Mrs. Willis was reading some portions of scripture to him he said, "Dearest, I love you, oh so much, God only knows how much, but I love Jesus more. My love for him is different, a grander love. And now if he is calling me home I commend you and my dear baby boy Ossian to His infinite shepherding care, to lead and keep you forever."

One day while Mrs. Willis was trying to soothe him in his restlessness he was looking most earnestly off into space, and a strange expression came over his face, he seemed radiant with joy. Turning suddenly toward her he said, "Dearest now I know what the love of Jesus is, the door is open wide." His last request was that if his dear wife should reach home and her health and strength permit she should take up the evangelistic work to "win souls for Christ" and also plead the cause of Africa. He sank rapidly and his sufferings seemed to increase with his prostration until near midnight Sunday August 30, 1885, when the sacred hush fell upon all. The little room was filled with a hallowed presence, strangely sad yet beautiful and sweet. How long it remained the sorrowful watcher may never tell but ere it passed away the holy kiss of peace was placed upon the brow of the sleeping saint. His sufferings were over and he had pillowed his weary head on Jesus breast and entered into his eternal rest. To him there was no dark valley of death, no deep waters of Jordan, for his light and life of love glided calmly and sweetly into the grander light and life of Christ. It was indeed "Good night on earth and good morning in Heaven." Brother Willis was not, for God took him.

His last words were "Dearest the door is open wide." "O! the gate is open wide and the glory is just ahead; Hallelujah to Jesus."

Weary with suffering and worn with anxiety and care, sister Willis by this additional stroke seemed truly heart-broken. Half dazed she counted the moments as they flitted by. With her life almost crushed with a sorrow which knew no bounds, and her sweet baby boy tugging at her heart strings; her devoted husband sleeping in death by her side, and she thousands of miles from home on storm tossed seas, fainting and ready, yea anxious to die, she moaned in anguish of spirit and found comfort only in Him " Who weeps o'er other's woes " Jesus gave her rest and peace and imparted fresh strength for the sorrowing hour. His death made a profound impression upon all on board. Officers and crew at that midnight hour stood with uncovered heads and tearful eyes, in the presence of his lifeless form. The next day the burial took place about seven A. M. The steamer was stopped for a few moments and amid the solemn stillness that followed the body of Rev. H. M. Willis was consigned to its ocean sepulcher to await the day when "The earth and the sea shall give up their dead."

Some conception of her confident trust in Christ amidst the thick darkness which had settled down upon her may be gathered from a clipping from her journal written the day after the death of Brother Willis. " August 31— My precious husband passed triumphantly through the portals last evening. Glory to Jesus for victory over death. No one but the Master knows how deep is the wound, for I loved him most dearly. If he was away from me an hour I grew restless, and my heart seems crushed when I glance at the future, but I praise the Lord, the Comforter is mine.

'Saviour I come like a poor wounded dove,
And my head I would lean on thy bosom of love.'

The dear tenement of clay was lowered into the deep this morning about seven o'clock but *he* had entered into rest."

The remainder of the voyage was a mingling of suffering and sorrow, now and then a gleam of sunshine, but many and thick were the shadows. Each morning brought fresh trials and each setting sun gilded the mountain tops of Faith's victories. As the Biafra was grandly riding the waves of the sea, so Mrs. Willis was lifted above every wave in life's ocean for underneath her were the Everlasting arms, and here she found a refuge and a rest.

She cannot find words to express her gratefulness to Captain Thomas, and his kind officers and men, who did so much for her in those hours when friends were beyond price. Thousands of christian people join her as she expresses her thankfulness in fervent prayers for these faithful men. On reaching Liverpool she was so ill that no one thought she could ever recover, nor even be able to start for her Western home. Fowler Brothers learning of her arrival in the city promptly came to her aid and did all in their power to relieve her every want. She holds in grateful remembrance the many kindnesses received from them ; a debt of love the blessed Master will surely pay. Through skilful treatment and careful nursing the Lord granted her renewed strength and when sufficiently recovered she took passage on the steamship "Servia" of the Cunard line for New York. The voyage was truly a sad one, but her face was turned toward home and hope cheered her fainting heart. She landed in safety on Monday, September 28, 1885, weak and exhausted, and with baby tired and fretful. She went at once to the home of Mrs. Fleming, a dear lady of her acquaintance and found loving, sympathizing friends, who gave every attention, and royally welcomed her to their hearts and home. It was yet feared that she might not live to get home in Ohio. Remaining at New York two days she then proceeded to Philadelphia, where she arrived among her friends of Norris Square M. E. Church. Dear ones were waiting at the train to bid her welcome and the carriage of Mr. Johnson conveyed her to his home where everything that could be done for her welfare and personal comfort was done. Rev. Robt. F. Y. Pierce, Mr. Geo. M. Harkness, who had worked so earnestly with Brother and Sister Willis during their revival services in Norris Square Church, and many other friends called to extend their sympathies and render such assistance as they were able. As Sister Willis decided to remain over the Sabbath (October 4) among these friends, hoping to gain strength for the journey to her home in Ohio, the pastor of Norris Square M. E. Church, Rev. Thomas Harrison, suggested the propriety of holding a memorial service to Brother Willis on Sabbath evening. The friends unanimously approved of such a meeting and Mrs. Willis consented to be present during the service should her health permit. The announcement of this service, it is said, drew forth at an early hour a crowd that filled the Church, blocked up the doors, and extended even into the streets, hundreds in the meanwhile going away unable to get near enough to hear anything that might be said. With Mrs. Willis, the day set for the memorial service, was spent in much prayer that God would sustain and give her strength, for as she records,

"None knew how great a trial it would be for me to enter Norris Square Church without my precious husband at my side; nor what a sad rush of memories would flood my soul. Oh the anguish of spirit, God only knows how torn and bleeding is my heart." On the arrival of the hour for the memoral service, Mrs. Willis was escorted to the Church by the pastor and wife and the board of trustees of the Church. She entered the house with weak and faltering steps, almost over-borne with the weight of sorrow, but the divine Comforter and Helper was present to support and sustain and cheer.

The pastor, Brother Harrison, conducted the service and preached a sermon full of the Spirit of Christ. He chose as his text the words so appropriate to the life of our departed friend and brother. "For before his translation he had this testimony, that he pleased God."— Heb. xi: 5.

After an appropriate and tender discourse, Mrs. Willis was introduced and spoke a few words. The *Philadelphia Methodist*, October 10, 1885, speaks of this part of the service as follows:

"Sister Willis, who, throughout the service, occupied a place within the altar rail, then stepped upon the platform, and with a face bearing the marks of both mental and physical suffering, and yet at times beaming with hope and holy joy, in a most touching manner spoke of the work in Africa, of its success and glorious outlook and of the regret with which she had been compelled to leave it. Instead of being discouraged and disappointed as some of the secular papers had represented, the missionaries of Bishop Taylor, to a man, were full of enthusiasm and hope, and she herself, notwithstanding all she had suffered, would gladly go back to Africa if her health would permit. Her testimony to the value of religion and the sufficiency of divine grace for every emergency in life, was most touching, and few who heard her could doubt her sincerity, or question the truthfulnesss of her statements." The service throughout was one of the most impressive and solemn ever held in Norris Square Church. The tenderest sympathy was expressed by all in that large audience. The occasion will be long remembered by all who were present.

CHAPTER XX.

Memorial Window.—The kind people of Norris Square M. E. Church.—Mrs. Willis' stay in Philadelphia.—Her visit to the Methodist Episcopal Ministers' meeting.—Resolutions of sympathy.—Mrs. Willis departs for the home of her parents in Ohio.—The death of her father-in-law—The end of the history of the subject of this memoir.

Besides these expressions of regard and appreciation of the character and services of Brother Willis, the Norris Square Church did more. A kind brother of the society, John Branson, had learned to love and esteem Brother Willis for his faith and works among the people of Norris Square, and was wondering in his own mind what he might do to keep his name fresh and to make it a perpetual help to those who gave their hearts to God through his instrumentality. He thought of a memorial window. The Church building was just then being repaired and enlarged and an opportunity of the kind was readily afforded. Brother Branson accordingly asked the official board for the privilege of putting in a memorial window for Brother Willis. The request was granted, and a very handsome window, dedicated to his memory, now has a place in Norris Square Methodist Church of Philadelphia. This kind people whom the Lord raised up to aid Brother and Sister Willis in the work of the Lord, and especially in this outfit for Africa were ready to provide for the temporal wants of Mrs. Willis and child on their return, and, in an abundant way they helped and comforted her after the death of her husband so that in them she found the Lord supplying all her needs.

During her stay in Philadelphia, Mrs. Willis was able to attend the Methodist Episcopal ministers' meeting of the city which was held at the Methodist Book rooms, on the next morning after the memorial service. Here she was introduced to the brethern, and although weak from the extraordinary efforts required of her on the previous day, she addressed the meeting. Of her address in this meeting the *Christian Witness* of October 15th says ; " She spoke very intelligently and hopefully of Bishop Taylor's work. She says, Africa back of the coast line is a beautiful country and its poor benighted inhabitants are glad to hear of Jesus and his soul-satisfying religion. The harvest truly is great but the laborers are few. The address of Mrs. Willis in relation to Bishop Taylor and his work made a profound impression upon the ministers present, and every one that heard the intelligent utterances of this excellent sister, who had sacrificed all but life itself in this work, will think more kindly of the Bishop and his devoted companions and pray more fervently for their success in the " Dark Continent." "

The following resolutions of sympathy and condolence were read and adopted by the meeting before the close of its session:

Resolutions adopted by the Methodist Episcopal Preachers' meeting of Philadelphia and vicinity at their regular meeting, October 5, 1885.

"We deeply sympathize with our Sister Mrs. Anna Willis, who has been called to pass through a terrible affliction in the loss of her husband, the Rev. H. M. Willis, who was on his way from his missionary work under Bishop Taylor in Africa, to bring his wife to this country in order that she might regain her health and return with reinforcements to Africa.

We commend our dear sister and her child to the affectionate regard of the Church and above all to the Great Head of the Church, who hath said, "I will never leave thee nor forsake thee."

The above resolutions were introduced by Rev. T. A. Fernley, and unanimously adopted.

ALEX. M. WIGGINS, *President.*
ALPHA G. KYNETT, *Secretary.*

THOMAS HARRISON, *Attest.*

After a few days stay with her friends of Norris Square Church, Mrs. Willis left Philadelphia on Sunday, October 6th, for the itinerant home of her parents, now at Mt. Hope, Holmes county, Ohio, where her father was pastor of the M. E. Church. She and her little son Ossian arrived on the next day and were greeted with more than ordinary tenderness by father and mother and kindred dear, and in every way were made most welcome to their home and hearts. Here she heard for the first time of the death of her father-in-law, Mr. Dedrick Willis, who had died at his home in Ashland, O., on the 31st of August, just one day after her husband had passed away. She at once visited her mother-in-law and her husband's relatives at Ashland, the childhood home of Mr. Willis. She found them, too, in deep affliction over the double loss they had sustained. After a brief stay at Ashland, Mrs. Willis returned to her father's home where she spent a short time in rest, recruiting her health and strength that she once more might be of service in the Master's vineyard.

We have now come to the end of the history of the subject of this memoir. The career of Rev. H. M. Willis is now ended. The work assigned him is finished. He has done what he could to save men. His labors have been fruitful for good on both sides of the sea. He lived not for self but for Christ, whose seal he bore, and whose blessings followed him everywhere, and whose grace sustained him in life and in the hour of death. He won great victories in the name of the Lord in the evangelistic field, so that thousands of souls will point to him as the instrumentality in their salvation. He was all the Lord's and all the years of his future was consecrated to His service. But in the wisdom of God he was ripe for heaven and in early life God took him. The sea became his winding sheet. We cannot explain, but may it not be that he is one of those who will live after they are dead, and that his ocean grave may become his pulpit from which to speak to the souls of men. May it not be that from this pulpit he can penetrate further in behalf of Christ and the unsaved millions, than from any pulpit from which he ever preached.

For some wise end God has called our brother and he is among us no more. His body rests in the sea of a foreign clime. His last memorial is said and we now bid good-bye to our departed brother who lived so purely, accomplished so much and died so nobly in the great cause for which his life was given.

We now turn our thoughts from Brother Willis, and for one more brief chapter, invite the attention of the reader, to his companion, who has lived to reach home from the Dark Continent and again to unfurl the banner of the Lord in the evangelistic work of this her own native land.

CHAPTER XXI.

Mrs. H. M. Willis.—By Nature an Evangelist.—Her gifts known to her Husband.—His dying request for her to continue the Work.—Her safe return to America.—The Salvation of Souls dearer than Life.—Her brief Rest.— The opening of the Way.—Calls to Evangelistic Services.— NORRIS SQUARE, signal success.—Fever and Prostration.—Rest and Recovery.—Ready for Duty.—NORTH WALES, a Good Meeting.—TRINITY, NEW YORK. Her Impressive Sermons.—Her Modesty and Simplicity.— The Wonderful Display of God's Power.—A Glorious Revival—Her return to Ohio.—Greets her Boy.—A Short Rest.—Returns to Philadelphia.—North Fourth Street Union Mission.—Anywhere to save souls.—The Pastor's Report.— The Jubilee Service.—Rejoicing and Testimony of many Converts.—Mrs. Willis greatly appreciated.— An Account of her Life Work.—Suffers still from African Fever and Nervous Prostration.—Compelled to rest.—Cancels many Engagements—Returns to Ohio for the Summer.—Attends, Summer Assemblies.—Expects to continue the Evangelistic Work.—Closing Remarks.

Mrs. Anna Willis, the surviving companion of Rev. H. M. Willls, was an evangelist by nature, inducted into the office and confirmed by the Holy Ghost. In the former part of this work we have already given a leaf from her history, and now have only to speak of her separate evangelistic labors and life, after the death of her husband, whom she loved so tenderly and with whose life and work, during their union, she was so closely identified.

Her husband well knew the rare qualities and gifts with which she was endowed as a special agent in winning souls. After he was stricken down at sea, and it became apparent to his own mind, that the hour of his departure was at hand, his dying request was, that if Mrs. Willis should reach home, and her health should be sufficiently regained, she should give herself to the work of an evangelist; and as she would have opportunity plead the cause of Africa. This request was in keeping with her own purpose and desire. She desired to save souls and could scarce be restrained.

On arriving home, though weak in body and suffering much from African fever, and also from the nervous shocks through which she had just passed, she could not wait long before engaging in the actual work of an evangelist. Her physician thought her health to be in a very critical condition and would not encourage her to undertake any work, for he was doubtful whether she would live through the coming winter. But she felt that God had yet a great work for her to do, and firmly believed that He would give her strength to perform it. She felt that she might not have a great while to work and could not think of allowing the campaign, just opening for revival work to pass by unimproved. The opportunities for such evangelistic services open before her as in earlier days. She heard the calls of her Master in the line of her chosen work from various quarters, and among others an invitation to hold a revival service in the Methodist Episcopal Church of Norris Square, Philadelphia, where something like a year before she had joined her husband in his last great revival, just before their departure for Africa. Here the same esteemed brother, Rev. Thomas Harrison was pastor and the same dear people sustained the work. This invitation Mrs. Willis accepted as her first work after returning from the missionary field, and after the wonderful experiences in the same.

Leaving her boy now with her parents in Ohio, she reached Norris Square, on Wednesday November 18, 1885. The meetings began on the following Sunday, November 22. She had fasted and prayed for souls. Her faith staggered not at the promises of God. The Holy Ghost was poured out upon the Church and the people. The first day was a great victory, the Church receiving a new impetus for the work of the Lord, and a great baptism of divine power.

At night notwithstanding the disagreeable weather and the rain that commenced in the afternoon and continued throughout the evening, the congregation was large—every seat in the audience room being occupied and the class-rooms thrown open. The power of God was upon the evangelist in a wonderful degree. There was a great weeping in the congregation and many came to the altar, and a number sought Christ in other parts of the house. The revival indeed was already begun. From day to day the work went on, and progressed, and souls of almost all classes were saved, and whole families were converted to God. Among those who sought Christ in this meeting, we mention one man who, while under the influence of liquor, sought an interview with the evangelist. She found indeed that he was under deep conviction, and prayed with him. He bowed at the altar that same evening and was saved. Just after his visit, Mrs. Willis in company with another lady of the Church started out to seek the wife of the inquirer. They found her in a house furnished quite comfortably, but traces of rum could be seen. These Christian workers prayed and talked with the poor heavy hearted woman, and with tears streaming down her cheeks she said she would like to be a Christian. She came to the meeting and was very happily converted, and looking up she praised God aloud. With this husband and his wife, many families were made to rejoice on account of the great work of God in their uplifting and salvation.

Though quite feeble in health and sometimes quite prostrated by attacks of fever, during the course of the meeting, the evangelist continued in this work at Norris Square for something more than two weeks, when through failing health she was unable to continue the meetings. She was threatened with typhoid fever, and her physician insisted that if she continued to work, it would be at the risk of her life. It was a great task for her to close a meeting that was in such a good condition. On the last Sunday night twenty persons were at the altar seeking salvation, and nineteen had come there for the first time. The awakening spirit was on the people and God was crowning all the work with abundant success, but the evangelist could work no longer, and the meetings were closed. More than fifty were added to the Church.

With due care and needed rest the threatened attack on Mrs. Willis' health was averted. On a page of Mrs. Willis' journal written at that time she says: "I needed these few days of rest very much. I feel that while the body has been resting I have been increasing in the knowledge and wisdom of God. I am also much improved in health, and thus better prepared to work for the Master. Glory to Jesus!"

Her next engagement to hold revival services was with the Methodist Episcopal Church at North Wales, Montgomery Co., Pa., with Rev. H. Hess, pastor. Here special meetings began Sunday morning, December 27, 1885. From the beginning the blessing of the Lord attended the work. At the first service the evangelist was seconded during the preaching by some very hearty amens. Many bowed at the altar railing and at several front pews seeking a special baptism of the Holy Ghost for service. The Holy Spirit soon came upon the Church, and the power of the Lord was manifest to all. In the afternoon a special revival Sunday-school service was held. The services were very impressive; many were melted to tears, and a large number arose for prayers. Conversions began to take place, and the time of rejoicing and revival was at hand. The Lord was with his people and the work moved on.

The evangelist recognized the difficulty of this field in revival work, and stated that nothing less than the power of God would arouse the people. She looked to the One, who is mighty to save, to awaken the people of this community and to send a great revival before the meeting closed.

From that day the meetings increased in interest and power. The Church was greatly revived, and sinners were awakened and converted. Some professed holiness and many were greatly advanced in the Christian life. After about ten days of faithful work the meetings closed with great success, and the Church and people were made to rejoice on account of the salvation and blessings received.

That the reader may obtain a better knowledge of the work at this place and at the same time catch a glimpse of the spiritual life of the one whom God so highly honored in the work of the salvation of souls, we here close the history of the meeting at North Wales with a few extracts clipped from her private journal recorded while engaged in the meetings of that place. Under date of December 31, 1885, she records her experiences and reflections in the following language: "On this last day of the old year, as memory's eye look back over the year that is just passed, recalling, now scenes of joy, and again scenes of conflict in a foreign field, and sorest grief, I can but cry God moves in a mysterious way. But looking over all that is passed, I feel no murmur arise, for I am sure that Jesus would not have led me through the fiery furnace, if it had not been the very best thing that could happen me for his glory. All things work together for good to them that love God." I know that I love him with all my heart, and he will not willingly afflict his child. I find that my sad experience has helped many to a life of entire consecration. I feel for those in sorrow, and have a sympathy for them I never knew before.

> Affliction's blast hath made me learn;
> To feel for other's woes,
> And humbly seek with deep concern
> My own defects to know."

Yesterday I received a letter from Africa. It made me feel afresh my loss, and I fell on my knees in an agony of tears, and while I talked with Jesus a sweet comfort filled my soul.

The meetings are increasing in interest, the church is being greatly revived, and sinners are being converted. Some have professed holiness and a goodly number are seeking it. Glory to God in the highest."

Under date, Jan. 4, 1886: " Received a call from Trinity M. E. Church, New York, this morning, I have a number of pressing calls—may the Lord direct me to his glory. Yesterday morning the Holy Ghost was so heavy upon me while delivering the message to the people that I came to my room exhausted. I felt as if wrapped in a flame of glory. O hallelujah! The windows of heaven were opened and such blessings fell on the congregation that many were not able to conceal their emotions. Last night was a night of victory for God. Glory to his name! As each moment passes I learn more and more of the length and breadth, and depth, and height, of the love of Christ."

> "My soul has found the land of rest
> The land of perfect holiness.
> Now Holy Spirit guide me on
> Until the glorious crown be won."

Closing the meetings at North Wales, Pa., Mrs. Willis now accepted an invitation to hold revival services at Trinity M. E. Church, Second Street, New York, with Rev. Thomas Birch, D. D. as pastor. Here the meetings began on Friday evening, January 15, 1886, under the most favorable auspices. The Church received the early as well as the later rains. On the first Sabbath morning the glory of God filled the house and a grand work was accomplished for the Master. In the evening

Trinity M. E. Church, N. Y. City

twenty-one responded to the call for penitents, by bowing at the altar, and a number more arose for prayers in the congregation. At the opening of these meetings the evangelist records in her journal some facts that may to some extent explain the wonderful and immediate results of this meeting, as well as those in other fields where she had labored. She says: "I am holding on to God for a special season of power in this Church. I like to be alone with God most of the time; for I find that it is by frequent communion with the blessed Trinity that I gather power for active public services. I can see myself growing in the divine life." And though he is ever filling me,—

> "Insatiate to this spring I fly;
> I drink, and yet am ever dry;
> Ah! who against thy charms is proof?
> Ah! who that loves can love enough?"

More and more do I realize how blessed it is to bask in the sunshine of perfect love.

> "O glorious hope of perfect love!
> It lifts me up to things above;
> It bears on eagle's wings;
> It gives my ravished soul a taste,
> And makes me for some moments feast
> With Jesus' priests and kings."

My soul doth exceedingly magnify the Lord this morning that I was ever led from living at a poor dying rate, to the land of Beulah. It is indeed to my soul

> "A land of corn and wine and oil,
> Favored with God's peculiar smile,
> With every blessing blest;
> There dwells the Lord our righteousness.
> And keeps his own in perfect peace
> And everlasting rest."

I am glad that there remaineth a rest for the people of God, and that we that believe do enter into rest. I like the present tense of " do enter in," because it does away with the idea that I must wait until I get to heaven before I can have heart rest.

> "Every day my hopes brighter,
> Though the hopes of earth are gone;
> Every day my rest draws nearer
> As my Saviour leads me on."

O, what an experience I am enjoying by simply trusting.

> " Trusting as the moments fly,
> Trusting as the days go by;
> Trusting Him whate'er befall,
> Trusting Jesus, that is all."

Certainly, here the harvest was ripe and ready to be gathered. People were so anxious to be saved that sometimes the evangelist did not get a chance to preach. On one evening while the congregation was singing one of the opening hymns, a woman weeping bitterly came to the altar. The altar services were then opened and others immediately followed. Among the number was an officer of the House of Refuge, a man advanced in years. In less than a week it was evident that the revival was taking on large proportions, and the altar began to be filled with penitents from night to night; cold hearted professors began to be aroused, while the earnest ones sought a greater baptism of the Holy Spirit. Each night was a night of victory and rejoicing. One evening a dear woman, after she was converted, looked up into the face of the evangelist, and with tears of rejoicing streaming down her cheeks said: " O, Mrs. Willis, may I bring my husband here to-morrow night?" " The work spread from heart to heart, and the fire of revival was kindled. The pastor encouraged and helped the noble work by his aid and direction. The evangelist was clothed with power, and dealt with the word of God as something real. She records in her journal: " At times I feel carried away with a mighty inspiration. Oh, what a hallowed influence surrounds me! How the breezes of paradise fan my soul as the Holy Spirit tenderly broods over me. O, that I could explain this feeling of holy inspiration that comes upon me as I stand between the living and the dead to urge sinners to repentance and Christians to take higher grounds.

Sometimes my whole being is so thrilled that I tremble under the mighty power of God as shock after shock reaches me from the heavenly battery. Oh! Hallelujah! At times a great hush comes over my soul until it quivers with hallowed peace and glory."

The revival here took hold of the Sunday-school. The excellent superintendent and teachers helped on the work and God blessed the school until most of the pupils were saved Thus the work went on. The second Sabbath was greater in results than the first, and the revival increased. But before the third Sabbath Mrs. Willis' strength gave away, and right in the midst of this increasingly glorious work at Trinity she was stricken with severe illness, and as soon as she was able she started for her home, in Eastern Ohio, to secure a few days of much needed rest.

The results of the meeting were glorious. A friend in writing of this work to Mrs. Willis a few weeks afterward said: "I wish you could have been here yesterday morning. I never saw such a sight in my life. When

Mr. Burch gave the invitation for all who wished to join the church on probation to come forward, eighty-three responded—four rows of people around the altar, and extending to the ladies' parlors. He had the official brethren come to the altar and shake hands with them. I never saw a congregation so moved. There was not a dry eye in the church. Old men as well as the young, at the altar and all around the house wept like babes. If there was such rejoicing on earth what must it have been in heaven. There were old gray haired men and their wives among the probationers, and many young men and women, husbands, and wives, and children. I never saw Mr. Burch so affected; it seemed as though he would not be able to go through with the services. There were about forty more who were not able to be present who said that they would join on probation. So you see your labor has not been in vain in the Lord.

In the columns of one of the religious weeklies of New York some further observations concerning the work and service of Mrs. Willis in this meeting at Trinity have been made, and as no more true, terse or expressive language can be found, we conclude this chapter by giving the reader the benefit of the article as taken from the paper. The paper states:

"The Church is passing through a precious revival, such as it has not had for years. The membership have long prayed for the outpouring of the Holy Spirit upon the congregation and community. God has, most graciously, answered prayer. There have been, recently, most wonderful displays of God's power in the salvation of the people. The old, middle-aged and young, have knelt side by side at the altar, and have testified that they were saved. The membership has been quickened and have stood together in the work.

For two weeks the Church has had the benefit of the services of Mrs. Anna Willis, a missionary lately returned from Africa. God has blessed her labors wonderfully. Her appeals have been stirring, and pointed directly at the hearts of the unconverted. Some of the texts she used we shall never forget. Some that we remember particularly are these: "And the door was shut;" "Is your heart right;" "And there is a Friend that sticketh closer than a brother;" "Beloved, now are we the sons of God, and it doth not yet appear what we shall be; but we know that, when He shall appear, we shall be like Him, for we shall see

Him as He is;" "Come unto Me all ye that labor and are heavy laden, and I will give you rest." Mrs. Willis is a fluent speaker and very earnest. We have heard several lady evangelists, but none have impressed us by their modesty and simplicity as she did. Her whole heart is in the service of her Master, and she impresses her hearers with the fact that she is working solely for their good. She came to Trinity a perfect stranger, but left with the esteem and well-wishes of the congregation. She returns home to Ohio, her native State, to spend a few days in rest. She suffers still from the African fever, contracted on the coast of Africa last summer. Her next engagement will be in Philadelphia. Many will arise in heaven and call her blessed. She certainly, by her winning way, has subdued hearts that have passed through several revivals untouched, and who have, through her instrumentality, been led to Jesus. Her good work in Trinity will never be forgotten. Personally, we are better for having listened to the wonderful appeals of this estimable lady, and have no hesitancy in recommending her to any Church who may be privileged to gain her services. We bid her God speed in her work of love. We hope to shake hands with her in the celestial city.

Leaving New York, as soon as she was able after her work at Trinity M. E. Church, Mrs. Willis went to her father's home at Mt. Hope, Ohio, for a brief rest and to visit her boy and dear ones at home. The scene of again meeting and parting is so beautifully portrayed in the journal of Mrs. Willis that we here give it in her own recorded words as follows: " As soon as I was able I started for my home in Ohio; had a severe chill on the way but arrived home safely. As I rode up to the door a bright little face was looking for me, while with a joyous voice my black eyed darling, in his own baby language, cried, "There's my mamma—there's my mamma." Oh, those days of sweet comfort with my sweet baby and dear ones. And there were moments of intense heart aches when my little darling would wind his arms about my neck and looking lovingly into my face would say: "Mamma has come home to take Ossie to heaven to see his papa." Sometimes after lisping his little prayer he would add: " and take Ossie soon to heaven to see his papa, for Jesus' sake."

" My mother heart would be crushed with sorrow as tender memories floated to me from the past. But those days only too quickly passed, and clasping my little one to my heart with all a fond mother's yearnings, and pressing a good-bye kiss on his baby lips I started out again through blinding tears on my mission for my Master."

Her next revival work was to be at the John B. Stetson Union Mission on North Fourth Street, Philadelphia, with the Rev. Robert F. Y. Pierce in charge, who on request has kindly furnished a faithful and graphic account, which, instead of attempting a description ourselves, we here give to the readers. This account is as follows:

REV. BROTHER SIMMS:

It gives me great pleasure to bear testimony to the faithful labors of one who is trying to do so much for our blessed Lord and Master.

The harvest may not have been so large in point of members as other fields may report in which she has toiled, but when one is familiar with the peculiarity of our mission work there must be a hearty "Praise God" burst forth in acknowledgment of a wonderful work of grace.

The North Fourth Street Union Mission of Philadelphia was organized in January, 1880, by Mr. John B. Stetson, hat manufacturer; a wealthy and philanthropic gentleman, who, in remembrance of his boyhood days spent in the

Sabbath school desired to benefit the children of, and the employees of his factory. He was not a professing Christian, but one who realized the leadings of Providence. One of the rooms of the factory was opened and the first Sunday seventy-five registered their names. Mr. Hampson was chosen Superintendent, and has ever since ably filled the position. The room soon became too small to accommodate the growing attendance and other rooms were opened.

Three years ago a room large enough to accommodate several hundred was erected adjoining the factory, simply for Sunday-school and mission work. So greatly had the work been blessed that Rev. Robert F. Y. Pierce was invited to take the management of it in November, 1884. Preaching services were at once instituted and a precious revival soon followed.

This new building was now too small and it was greatly enlarged during the Fall of 1885. Before it was completed and dedicated, Sister Willis was invited to conduct a series of revival meetings. The school now numbers nearly 1100 and between 300 and 400 earnest Christian workers are found among the teachers and older scholars, Mr. Stetson himself having recently been brought to a saving knowledge in Christ. We have no Church or other organization with us but conduct our work on the broadest evangelistic methods possible. Our converts are promptly urged to unite with the Christian Churches of their choice about us, but they are not lost to us.

To this peculiar work our sister was invited and came with the blessing of God. She was weary in body and suffering from a severe attack of the African fever together with a recent cold, but on Sabbath afternoon, February 14th, she held up Christ to our school and invited each member to come to the fountain opened for all. In the evening she presented Jesus, the sinners friend, to a large congregation and at the close of the service thirty-five sin-sick souls were crying out for mercy. In consequence of an attack of quinsy and African fever Mrs. Willis was compelled to desist for a time from labor. It must be remembered that in all this work there was no Church organization to aid in the work ; and no official members to share in the responsibility. Several persons kindly assisted when not engaged with their own Church work, but during the weeks which followed Mrs. Willis was practicaly unaided except by the pastor, who, through the blessing of God was an efficient help. Sabbath evening, February 21,

Mrs. Willis resumed the service and for the three weeks following, she labored to win souls for Christ.

Over 150 were brought to Christ during these meetings and we look upon them as the harbinger of better days yet to come. The inspiration lingers and the good work still goes on. Every prayer meeting night six or eight have been numbered with our enquirers.

We regard Mrs. Willis as a woman of remarkable power, and love her for her simplicity of Christian character and beauty of childlike faith. She lives near her Saviour, so that in every day duties, as well as into every public service, she brings Jesus. Many will rise up to call her blessed when she shall have entered into the joy of her Lord.

Faithfully yours,
ROBERT F. Y. PIERCE.

In addition to this terse, and careful report, we would also call attention to the fact that about the close of this meeting, a very beautiful account of the life of Mrs. Willis, from the pen of the same writer, appeared in the columns of the National Baptist, April 8, 1886, a paragraph or two from which we here quote for our readers: " A visit to the North Fourth

Street Mission, at Fourth and Montgomery Avenue, during the progress of the revival meeting conducted by Mrs. H. M. Willis, convinced one that the work of the Holy Spirit was truly wonderful, and that Mrs. Willis was a remarkable woman. Though young in years, she is old in trials and sorrows; though weak in body, she is strong in the Lord, and in the power and demonstration of the Spirit. Hundreds have been led to Christ, and she is never so happy as when speaking and working for him. Her manner is so simple and plain that one often wonders at the marvelous results of her preaching. But a knowledge of her inner life reveals the secret, for she knows " 'Tis not by might nor by power, but by my Spirit saith the Lord;" " hence she walks with God. In conscious nearness to him, she exemplifies that purity of character, that sweetness of Christian life which wins souls to her Lord. The African fever still troubles her, rendering her at times wholly unfit for service. By the positive demands of physicians and the earnest request of her many kind friends she has consented to rest for a few months. Would to God there were more just such laborers, willing, if needs be, to lay down their lives for Jesus sake."

The special services of North Fourth Street Mission, as further reports have shown, closed with a very impressive jubilee meeting, when those that had been led to Christ, during the meetings, rejoiced together and gave earnest testimonies and bright evidences of life and salvation never known before.

With this meeting of North Fourth Street Union Mission, in which so many new converts gave positive assurance of acceptance in Christ, Mrs. Willis closed her evangelistic labors for the season, and in accordance with the demands of physicians and the advice of friends she canceled her many engagements for further revival services and returned to her home in Ohio, where she is now resting in order to regain her health and energies that she may enter in the Fall with renewed strength, into other fields of work. During the Summer she may visit Chatauqua, Ocean Grove, and other of the great assemblies, but most of the time will be spent in the quiet home of her parents at Mt. Hope, Ohio, in company with father mother, sisters, and with her own little son Ossian. The moments will fly swiftly, and the time will soon come when she may go out again at the call of her Master to win other victories for her Lord; to spend and be spent for his glory. May it be the pleasure of the Lord to spare her many years for his great work of winning the unsaved to God, and may he grant that her future life may be as beautiful and Christ like as the past, and that with increasing strength and efficiency, she may continue the soul-saving work to which she has evidently been called, and for which, by the Holy Spirit, she has been so admirably equipped. With this record of events and facts along the pathway of these Christian evangelists we now come to the close of this volume. He, of whom we have spoken, has already finished his course and has gone on to enter through the gates into the city. She whose life and work we have briefly and imperfectly sketched, still lives to labor in the great harvest of soul-gathering, and, doubtless, in this work she will be found faithful unto death, and afterwards in heaven, with her husband and co-laborer. Rejoice with the thousands of saved souls whom they have won to Christ.

www.ingramcontent.com/pod-product-compliance
Lightning Source LLC
Chambersburg PA
CBHW031959230426
43672CB00010B/2211